I0079897

REFOCUS **REKINDLE** REJOICE

Pastor Tom Anglin! I just finished reading your book. You have great messages of encouragement and challenge the reader. I am sure this book will bring not only encouragement but, as well, the challenge to many readers. I pray that many people who read this book will be blessed, encouraged, and challenged to live a victory life for our Kingdom.

Dr. Paul Ai, President
Vision Outreach International

I have found your encounters with God to be very interesting and gripping. As a matter of fact, I could not stop reading!! I am convinced this devotional book is going to be a great success as well as a tremendous blessing to many people.

Dr. John Bosman, President and Chairman of the Board
Spirit Wind International

Tom Anglin has lived a life of miracles, with plenty of ups and downs along the way. Here he shares his personal story with total honesty, holding nothing back. And best of all, he does it in a practical, life-giving way. As you read of his encounters with the Spirit, your own faith will be enriched, and your own walk with God deepened. It's time to dive in deeper!

Dr. Michael L. Brown, President of FIRE School of Ministry
Host of the Line of Fire radio broadcast

Pastor Tom Anglin possesses a unique blend of fatherly wisdom and childlike faith. His heart shows through his writing, and this work is sure to bless you, just as it did me.

Rev. Casey Doss, Lead Pastor
Hope Unlimited Church, Knoxville, Tennessee

I have known Tom Anglin for over 30 years. He is called of God and a man who passionately loves the Lord. His life has been an awesome testimony to thousands over the years. He is a man of integrity and truly exhibits the "fruits and gifts of the Holy Spirit." This book is very down to earth, with many personal illustrations that paint a true picture of this man and his life. Truly a great read that will touch your heart.

Rev. Doug Hammond, Lead Pastor
First Assembly of God, Olivet, Michigan

Tom Anglin's book is much more than a quick read. It blends the experiences of his own journey with God's hand in the midst of it all. It is inspiring, encouraging, and thought provoking. I love the personal illustrations but, most of all, the poignant call at the end of each chapter to "Refocus Rekindle Rejoice." I found myself looking back on my own life and how God's hand has directed me. I know you will benefit from these devotionals.

Dr. Rick Ross, Superintendent
North Carolina Assemblies of God

This book is true to the promise of its title. These powerful accounts are not merely the experiences of a man of faith and his family. They are a clarion call of awakening to all who would dare to believe, "With God all things are possible!"

Rev. Stephen Smith, President
Times Of Refreshing Ministries

Tom, I read your book. It really is very inspiring, and I believe that many people will be blessed to read how, through your years of serving God, He has been faithful to you and your family. I believe our lives are meant to help others go through things we've already been through. Even to encourage parents that their children can be far from God, but prayer can always bring them home to the Father. Thank you for your openness to share with others.

Mrs. Pamela Taylor Stone
Perry Stone Ministries, Cleveland, Tennessee

Pastor Tom Anglin has been my spiritual father in the faith, and a great friend, for the past 25 years. Tom is a man full of The Holy Ghost, wisdom, revelation, faith, passion, and of power in Christ. He has a burden to reach the lost, at any cost. This book will encourage you in your faith and will challenge you in your walk as you read about Tom's spiritual journey and about God's faithfulness in the midst of that journey.

Rev. James Turner
Urban Outreach Phoenix

This book from the heart of my friend, Tom Anglin, carries the footprint of Jesus all over it. I'm impressed with how Tom heard the voice of Jesus with clarity in everyday situations and how amazing His provision follows if we can listen well. An overwhelming awareness of His presence captured my heart reading this book. Tom Anglin carries the beat of His heart as I sensed it strongly in reading this book. Let the personal experiences in this book become a reality in your life. He is with us in everyday life situations, and this book will draw you into a renewed walk with Him with demonstrations of His Spirit as evidence He is with you all the time. Rejoicing will be your companion.

Rev. Andre Van Zyl, President
Good News To The Nations

I am happy to recommend Tom Anglin's small but largely impacting book. His personal story is very compelling, as well as the remarkable answers to prayer in his family's faith journey. I find the chapters to be inspiring and instructive. I personally have been blessed reading it.

Rev. Don Wilkerson, President
Teen Challenge, Inc. (Co-founder of Teen Challenge and Times Square Church NYC)

Tom Anglin has put together a warm-hearted, personal, and deeply encouraging devotional that will both challenge and bless you. I love Tom's honesty and clarity. You will find yourself in much of what he has experienced, and these writings will be a helpful guide in your life journey. I have known Tom for many years, and I know that these devotionals were written by a man after God's own heart.

Rev. Gary Wilkerson, President
World Challenge

As a Christian publisher, we appreciate the works that teach the body of Christ and meet special needs. Tom Anglin's book does that. It will have an impact in support settings for the addicted and also teaches and provides encouragement to those desiring a stronger faith life or a deeper, more obedient relationship with our Lord Jesus Christ. We are pleased to give "Refocus Rekindle Rejoice" a 5 STAR rating.

Nancy E. Williams, President
The Laurus Company, Inc.

REFOCUS
Rekindle
REJOICE

• REFOCUS YOUR VISION • REKINDLE YOUR FAITH
• REJOICE IN YOUR RENEWAL

TOM ANGLIN

FOREWORD BY KEITH HOLLOWAY

LAURUS BOOKS

Unless otherwise notated, all Scripture references are from the New King James Version®. Copyright © 1982 by Thomas Nelson, Inc. Used by permission. All rights reserved.

Scripture taken from the NEW AMERICAN STANDARD BIBLE, Copyright © 1960, 1962, 1963 1968, 1971, 1972, 1973 1975, 1977, 1995 by The Lockman Foundation. All rights reserved. Used by permission. http://www.Lockman.org

REFOCUS **REKINDLE** REJOICE

BY TOM ANGLIN

Copyright © 2018 by Tom Anglin

All rights reserved. This book is protected under the copyright laws of the United States of America. This book may not be copied or reprinted for commercial gain or profit. The use of short quotations or occasional page copying for personal or group study is permitted and encouraged. Permission will be granted on request.

Paperback: ISBN: 978-1-943523-55-9

Mobi (Kindle): ISBN: 978-1-943523-56-6

ePub (iBooks, Nook): ISBN: 978-1-943523-57-3

Cover Design by Maria Anglin

Original Cover Photo by Ian Keefe

Published by LAURUS BOOKS

LAURUS BOOKS
www.TheLaurusCompany.com

This book may be purchased in paperback from TheLaurusCompany.com, Amazon.com, and other retailers around the world. May also be available in formats for electronic readers from their respective stores.

DEDICATION

First of all, I would like to dedicate this book to my Lord Jesus Christ, without Whose immeasurable grace, mercy, kindness, and love I would have been long dead and suffering the torments of eternal Hell. To Him I owe all my love, and I declare that He alone is worthy. To know Him and to make Him known is my whole life's ambition.

Next, I would like to dedicate this book to the following people:

- My darling bride, Tammy. Since April 26, 1980, she has faithfully accompanied me through many dangers, toils, and snares. She is the bravest woman I have ever known. Her love and faithfulness to Jesus and myself are priceless. Oh, that I may truly love her as Christ loves His Bride. She has been my closest earthly friend and confidant. Tammy not only is an amazing wife, she is an incredible mother of four and grandmother of almost eight at the time of this writing.

• My four children, the joy of my life: Ryan Daniel, Sarah Danielle, Destiny Amber, and Tyler Evan-David. If I never did anything else in life but help to raise them and point them to Jesus, it would have been enough for me. They have been eyewitnesses to most of the testimonies written in this book. I am forever grateful to the Lord for blessing me with these wonderful men and women of God. I am confident that no Dad has ever been more proud of his children than I am of mine.

• My two sons-in-law and my two daughters-in-law: Maria, Gabe, Modesto, and Jordan. I could not be more blessed. They are as good as it gets. Their love for the Lord is so evident in the lives they lead. They were hand picked by the Lord to marry our kids.

• Have I told you about my six grandchildren? Well, let me just tell you that they delight my heart beyond words: Rylie Grace, Liam Edward, Naomi Corinne, Nolan Fisher, Elliot Jude, Caroline Elyse, and two more on the way at the time of this writing.

• My parents: My father, the late Thomas E. Anglin, Sr., and my precious mother, Evelyn Anglin, who is 91 at the time of this writing. These two people shaped my life like no others. Their love, prayers, and examples for me have blessed my life beyond words. I was given way better parents than I deserved.

• My sister, Kathy, and brother-in-law, Jeff. They took me into their home shortly after my return to Christ. They helped me onto the firm foundation of Jesus Christ. They have always shown me incredible love and kindness.

They are truly amazing disciples of Jesus Christ.

• The Godly heritage with which I was blessed. To my godly grandparents and great-grandparents, whose prayers have paved the way for my incredible journey with Jesus. How blessed I am.

• Last, but certainly not least, I dedicate this book to the congregations I have been privileged to pastor these last 32 years. I have loved them all very dearly. The Bridge Church of WNC, my home church. They have stood with me through thick and thin over this last decade. I love you all so much.

There is not enough time or space for me to include everyone I would like to recognize. There are so many dear family members and friends who have greatly impacted my life through the years. He knows them all. God bless them all.

ACKNOWLEDGEMENTS

Special Appreciation:

EDITING
Shaun Gillespie
Sarah Anglin McKinney
Diana L. Meadows

FOREWORD
Rev. Keith P. Holloway

REVIEWERS

Dr. Paul Ai
Dr. John Bosman
Dr. Michael L. Brown
Rev. Casey Doss
Rev. Doug Hammond
Dr. Rick Ross
Rev. Stephen Smith

Mrs. Pamela Stone
Rev. James Turner
Rev. Andre Van Zyl
Rev. Don Wilkerson
Rev. Gary Wilkerson
Rev. Nancy E. Williams

COVER DESIGN
Maria Anglin

COVER PHOTO
Ian Keefe

LOVE AND SUPPORT
Tammy Anglin
Ryan, Maria, Tyler, and Jordan Anglin
The Bridge Church of WNC

TABLE OF CONTENTS

FOREWORD

If you were ever to meet Pastor Tom Anglin, you would immediately identify a few key character traits that make this man a person of impact: first, his foundational deep love for Christ, next his heart-felt compassion for all people but especially fellow Christ-followers, and lastly, his sincere inspirational drive for seeing Christians encouraged in life through pursuit of the One who has called us into His eternal kingdom.

Pastor Tom is a people person who has more Biblical sayings, combined with a home-town country perspective that draws you into his circle of influence and likely the nearest coffee shop or restaurant. His motto of "man does not live by bread alone" will soon have you sharing your deepest thoughts and experiences over a fine meal somewhere. He is a sympathetic listener, whether it is his family, his church members, or the prison inmates he ministers to on a regular basis. He takes the input and runs it through a Biblical filter, along with his more than 30 years of ministry experience. What he then shares, much as in this exciting devotional book, will add value, inspiration, and clear direction to the needy. He will laugh and cry with you, tell you a story to bring a vital point home, and you'll know it's solid, that He is solid, and you'll be the better for it. You'll know he is a lover of Truth, an equal opportunity sharer of that Truth, which continues to teach and help him as well.

As you read the chapters of this challenging book, the reality and power of prayer will be easily seen; not prayers of liturgy but from a heart red hot for God, from one who was undone, lost without God and, yet, was drawn by Love to God's very heart and found salvation's solace.

Pastor Tom is a man of prayer that makes him an effective husband, father, pastor, and now author with conviction, consistency, and compassion. Every chapter is like peeling an onion, a sweet onion, as he lays himself, life, and truth honestly before every reader. Such genuine guidance is certainly worth more than the price of this book. If you aren't convinced or gripped by such practical yet spiritual realities, a second reading is most certainly warranted. This isn't simply a book to Pastor Tom. It is the display of the Almighty God and his Son, Jesus Christ, intersecting with broken, challenged, confused, and seeking souls. Walking together with a hungry humanity, Divinity instills Truth that is not intended to simply help but rather transform us to be as He is and then to live as He lived in our current broken societies to shine light to travelers in dark places.

Coming from a man I know and love, these deeply personal reflections will draw you in until you find yourself identifying with both a man and his God. By refocusing upward, rekindling inward, and rejoicing outward (the word literally means to "jump for joy"!) in an awesome God who takes life's ashes and brings forth new hope, you will truly be awakened to a living faith that our world is so desperately searching for.

> — Rev. Keith P. Holloway
> Senior Director
> World Poverty Solutions
> Colorado Springs, CO

REFOCUS

↓

REKINDLE

↓

REJOICE

PREFACE

"My sheep hear My voice, and I know them, and they follow Me. And I give them eternal life, and they shall never perish; neither shall anyone snatch them out of My hand."
— John 10:27-28

This little offering is written because I heard His voice say, "Begin to write your story of My faithfulness to you and your family."

My heart's desire is that **Refocus Rekindle Rejoice** would serve as an encouraging reminder to you that if you trust Him, He will most certainly lead you to green pastures, still waters, and the restoration of your soul. Our Great Shepherd and Bishop of our souls not only gives us eternal life in laying down His life for us, He also freely gives us all things. He gives us everything that pertains to life and godliness. He never fails the one who trusts Him.

I am an eyewitness to many miraculous happenings through my now 38 years of following His voice.

Faith is what pleases God. Great faith greatly pleases the Lord. Though this book's intent is a 21-day focus to stir and arouse your God-given measure of faith, it can certainly be read like any other book.

The world that you and I are living in is extremely distracting. There is so much to draw our attention away from the One who is worthy of our undivided attention. We must focus and refocus on Jesus. We must kindle and rekindle fervent prayer. I have found as I have practiced these two principles for many years, the outcome is always great reason for rejoicing.

I am certainly no special one. I am just a witness, a recipient, a beneficiary, an object of His great mercy and faithfulness. I declare to you that what He has done for us, He will certainly do for all who will call on Him.

Faithful is He who calls you, and He also will bring it to pass.
(1 Thessalonians 5:24 NASB)

~ Tom Anglin

1

Take Away The Stone

These things He said, and after that He said to them, "Our friend Lazarus sleeps, but I go that I may wake him up." Jesus said, "Take away the stone." Martha, the sister of him who was dead, said to Him, "Lord, by this time there is a stench, for he has been dead four days."

— John 11:11, 39

The passage of Scripture mentioned above depicts the story of Lazarus, a person who was extremely dead before Jesus called him back to life. In fact, he was so dead he stunk. That surely could have been said of me before Christ saved me. I heard a preacher once say, "You're dyin' from lyin', stinkin' from drinkin', and chokin' from smokin'." That was putting it lightly if one were to describe my lifestyle prior to salvation.

From the time I was thirteen years old, I became

proficient at partying and all aspects of a sinful lifestyle. I truly had forsaken the God of my childhood. I ran so far away from God that I felt that I was out of His reach and His love. My heart became like stone toward the Lord and the things concerning eternal life. I remember thinking one day, "I wish God would just go away and leave me alone." A horrible thought, I know, but that described my true feelings.

God did not go away, but the sense of conviction of sin greatly diminished in my life in a lot of ways. I was like a walking dead person rummaging through the garbage of this life, trying to gain some momentary pleasure with all that sin could offer. I was a true prodigal. Yet, I was a "fortunate son," born into a long line of praying people on both sides of my family, an heir to a godly heritage. My great-grandmother Styles, maternal grandparents, mother, big sister, and many others played a role in God's work in my life. These family members were truly my intercessors. They continually prayed for my soul, all the while not realizing how far I had strayed from the Lord. However, they knew that I was not where I needed to be, in fellowship with Jesus. Their prayers for me must have intensified.

By the time I was nineteen years old, very strange things began to happen to me. For example, I would drive to a remote place in the woods, smoke pot, and think about God. Another occurrence happened one night at work, when I was doing "window-pane acid" (LSD) and went into the restroom on my break. As I entered a stall, I saw that someone had written ugly words on the wall about another person. It turned my stomach. Without thinking it over, I took my pen and wrote in big letters: "JESUS LOVES YOU!" When I looked at it, I was shocked. The thought hit me, "Tom, you don't even believe He loves you. Why would you write that?" I did not have an answer, and without much more thought, I walked out of the restroom and went back to work.

My family was not only praying for me, they were soliciting other Christians to pray for me as well. Just like the stone that covered the tomb of Lazarus, the stone that covered my grave was beginning to tremble. Intercession was moving the stone, and conviction began to return to my heart. However, the stone had not yet been taken away. Oh, but thank the Lord for people who will pray and not give up.

By this time, my wife, Tammy, and I had started dating again. She liked to party, and we did a lot of that together. But something very strange happened. I told her that I did not want to get "high" with her anymore. She seemed surprised by my decision and asked, "What is happening to you?" She told me that I was changing and that she was concerned. I was deeply in love with Tammy, and I did not want to cause her any pain or harm.

One day, I sat down at my desk and thought about writing a song for a rock band that I was in at the time. I had no clue or inspiration of what to write. I heard the phrase, "Once you were free." I picked up my pen, and without giving it any further thought, I penned the following words:

Once you were free,
    as only His child could be.
But you shut your eyes to the true light
    because you didn't want to see.
You grew older and bolder
    and you turned your coldest shoulder
To the God
    you've always known was there.
O, but sooner or later,
    you're going to change your ways.
He loves you.
    He won't leave you alone.
Don't you realize
    that you're His child
And in Heaven
    He has made you a home?
He wants to set you free.
    Won't you let Him?
Let Him set you free!
    Free as only His child could be.
Open your eyes
    to the true light.
Won't you come and
    walk with Me?

My calloused heart was so cold and dead that I did not turn to the Lord, even though the Holy Spirit was obviously reaching out to me. I thought, "This is cool. Every band needs a religious song."

The long-suffering of Christ toward us is truly mind-boggling to say the least. The intercessors in my life kept praying, and the goodness of God kept working to lead me to repentance. As you will read later in Chapter 2, "Prodigal Awakening," His never-failing love broke through. Their prayers for me finally removed the stone that held my heart. Then Jesus cried with a loud voice, "Tom, come forth!" The son that was dead was alive again.

REFOCUS

Child of the living God, see Him again as the One who moves you to pray for the one who has gone astray.

REKINDLE

Ask the Holy Spirit to rekindle a fire of prayer in your own soul and the souls of others. Simply, I cannot say it better than this: "If I am a Christian, I am not set on saving my own skin, but on seeing that the salvation of God comes through me to others, and the great way is by intercession" (Oswald Chambers, *Disciples Indeed*).

REJOICE

When you offer yourself to the Great Holy Spirit, He will work through you with a mighty stone-moving power. Our responsibility, through intercession, is to roll away the stone that holds people captive in sin and separation from God. We do the rolling, and He will do the resurrecting. Rejoice because you are called to work with Jesus to raise the dead. Hallelujah!

REFOCUS

↓

REKINDLE

↓

REJOICE

2

Prodigal Awakening

"But when he came to himself, he said, 'How many of my father's hired servants have bread enough and to spare, and I perish with hunger!'"   — Luke 15:17

On February 22, 1979, I was deep in the muddy pig pen of sin. I had lost my focus and was on a journey to find myself in my own pursuit of happiness. That day in 1979, I went to the home of my sister and brother-in-law. I was always a little nervous when I was with them because they were strong Christians, and I felt like they could see right through me.

There was a constant weight of guilt that floated over me like a dark cloud, so it made our time together feel awkward. You see, I knew the truth. I knew about the Lord. I had met Christ through a powerful encounter at six years of age. From age six until around the age of thirteen, I tried to follow Christ as much as I understood how. And on that day in 1979, at the age of twenty, I was keenly aware that I had traveled far away from Jesus spiritually, and I felt miserably empty inside.

My sister, Kathy, constantly listened to Christian music. She was playing a song by Dallas Holm, a Christian singer-songwriter, when I arrived at her home. A phrase in the song caught my ear, "Give Him a year, starting today." It stunned me so much that I made a mental note to remember the date was February 22, 1979.

Even after that day, however, I continued with daily drug and alcohol abuse. It had become my normal way of life. I did not think much more about the lyric that caught my attention, nor the day of February 22nd. However, one year later to the date, at 4 a.m., Jesus came into me suddenly, and I came to my senses. He forever marked me that day.

I was alone in my car at that time, when He came rushing in. I could not help but turn back to Him with my whole heart as I experienced His incredible love and forgiveness. Later that evening, I remembered the phrase from that song. I was overcome with the awe of how the Lord had set the stage to bring me back to Him, exactly one year later to the date. I got my focus back, and I have determined never to lose it again. Now, 38 years later, He remains the center of my life and vision.

Dear reader, perhaps you have not blatantly or rebelliously turned away from Jesus as I did, but perhaps presently, you are not as focused on Him as you have been in times past. If so, there is good news. The Lord is right there with you to help you get your eyes back on

Him again. To be half-hearted or lukewarm about Jesus is a terrible waste of the life that Jesus has paid for with His own blood.

REFOCUS

Right now, come to your senses, and be honest with yourself. If you cannot look at yourself in the mirror and say that you are on fire for God, then just admit to God that you are lukewarm, and determine to make Jesus your total focus.

REKINDLE

Begin now to pray that God will give you a new focus on Him, and a new fire for Him in your soul. Soon, you will be on the road to discovering how great your Father's love is for you. With that growing revelation of His love that surpasses knowledge, you will be more and more in love with Him.

REJOICE

Oh, the things you will discover when you get your eyes completely focused on Him. He will lead you in paths of righteousness for His name's sake. The best is now yet to come. By faith, begin to praise and worship Him. The fire is going to burn!

REFOCUS

↓

REKINDLE

↓

REJOICE

3

I Love You, Too

… to know the love of Christ which passes knowledge;
that you may be filled with all the fulness of God.
— Ephesians 3:19

I shared in Chapter 2, "Prodigal Awakening," that I had an encounter with Jesus. I will share this encounter with you in more detail.

During this period of my life, before my encounter, I had drifted so far away from the Lord. I came to believe there was no way back to salvation, and I absolutely could not grasp the unconditional love of God.

Don't get me wrong. I was raised in a family that displayed unconditional love. In fact, my memories include my parents and my sister lavishing their love on me throughout my childhood. However, my problem was that they saw me as "Anglin, the Angel." But on the inside,

I was devilishly wicked.

I was raised believing that God knows everything, and I totally believed that. So knowing that He was a Holy God and saw everything, it was hard to think that He would and could love me. Several things happened to solidify that in my mind.

First, I had a dream that Satan came to my bedside in a black, hooded cloak. He had burning, ruby red eyes, and I was petrified! He motioned with his hand for me to follow him. Trembling, I got out of my bed, and fell on my knees. I pleaded with him that if he would not destroy me, I would do anything. Immediately, I awakened from the dream, and I was left feeling that I had just pledged my soul to the devil.

Second, shortly after this first dream, I had another dream where the Rapture was taking place, and many people around me were going up in the air to meet the Lord. I could not get off of the ground. In desperation, I climbed up onto a tree stump and jumped as high as I could off of it. I fell face first onto the ground. Again, I awakened terrified.

Finally, my fear was totally confirmed. My dreams were foretelling to the experiences I would soon face. One night in the summer of 1979, three of my closest friends and I went to a Black Sabbath concert. There, I had two encounters with the reality of Hell. Oh, friend, it is more real than I have ever heard it preached. I had been so wrong for far too long!

I was about to attend a concert of a lifetime, and I was so frustrated because we had only one pitifully impotent "joint" between the four of us. I did not even get high. I had been to many concerts, but never without being stoned. As one of the bands was playing, I began to feel so hot. The feeling became so intense that it felt like the building was on fire. I told my friends that the place felt like it was on fire. They told me that they were comfortable. In moments, the heat overcame me. I leaned up against the security wall right in front of the stage, and then I collapsed to the floor.

The floor broke through into a vertical tunnel, and I began to plummet downward. My hands and feet were chained together behind me. I was gagged and could not even scream. There was story after story of jail cells. The captives were screaming, "Don't come here! Go back! Go back!" I thought, "I would if I could!"

The farther I fell, the hotter it became. The heat was so powerful that I felt I would melt like wax. After falling for a long time, I could see a ring of fire. There in that fire were hideously frightening beast-like creatures. Hollywood could never create anything close to what I saw. They were so frightful looking I thought my heart would stop.

The creatures were dancing to the music that was playing in the concert above the portal I had fallen through. They were laughing hysterically at me and saying, "We have him now, we have him now!" They were reaching up to grab me as if they could not wait to get their claws and their fangs into me. Just as the tallest one was about to grab me, I was slapped back into the concert hall.

When I opened my eyes, my friends were panicked and screaming. They assumed that I was dead because I was so cold and lifeless. I was anything but cold. They threatened to call an ambulance. I shook my head to say no and motioned for them to leave me alone. I leaned back up against the wall. Immediately, I fell through the floor into the netherworld again. I had the same identical experience again. It was like an instant replay.

Meanwhile, back in the concert hall, my friends were now in a panic. I created such a scene, I was told later, that Manfred Man's Earth Band, the group that was playing, almost stopped their music. My friends thought I was already dead but continued to shake me, slap me, and scream at me. Just as someone turned to go and call for an ambulance, I came back to consciousness. I could not talk, and I could not walk. Two of my friends got underneath my arms and carried me over to the side with my feet dragging behind me. The people sitting there cleared out of the way so that I could sit down. After a few minutes, I could talk to my friends. It was like the horrifying experiences never happened. They asked me what had happened to me, and I said they would never believe me if I told them.

Black Sabbath was about to take the stage. I got up, and my friends asked me where I was going. I said, "I paid to see this band, and I am going to see them up close!" They all agreed that we should not return inside because something could happen to me again. I told them I was fine, and to suit themselves if they did not want to go with me, and off I went to the same area in which I had been standing earlier. Shortly thereafter, they made their way to me. I had no further incidents that night.

The next morning when I got up, my Mom met me in the hallway. She said, "Son, what happened to you last night?" I said, "Mom, you know that I went to a concert in Johnson City last night." Mom told me that she was aware of that. "But what happened at the concert, son?" she asked. I told her that it was great. "Why do you ask?" I inquired. With a terrified look in her eyes, she said, "I hadn't been asleep for long when the Lord woke me and said, 'You must pray for Tom, now!'" She went on to say, "I felt as though I was trying to pray you out of Hell itself."

I wanted to come clean about the double life I was leading, but I could not bring myself to tell her that she had prayed me out of Hell and the reasons why I deserved to go there. I just told her that I was thankful that she cared that much for me. Her experience rocked me more than even the experiences that I had the night before.

Even after that night, my heart was so hard that it was like it had not even happened. I began to drown my fears in alcohol and drugs more than ever. Partying was all that I had. I was going to an eternal Hell. I was so miserable that I wanted to die; however, at the same time, I did not want to go to Hell.

On another occasion, my friend, Junior Burke, and I were smoking pot in my car at 4 a.m. on February 22, 1980. Lightning struck a tree about fifty feet from where we were parked. The top of the tree exploded, and I said, "Talk about a light show!" Junior agreed. Then a thought hit me like a two-by-four between the eyes. I told Junior that I thought it should have been us instead of the tree. He asked what in the world I was talking about.

I said, "Well, look at us sitting here stoned in God's face." All I could feel in that moment was that God could not wait to throw me into Hell, a place that had become so real to me.

Junior told me that he had become a Christian several

years before and even felt called to preach. He, however, became discouraged and fell away from the Lord. He went on to say that he did not believe the Lord loved him anymore. I told him that was a ridiculous thing to say and that I knew God loved him.

Those words had barely left my lips when I heard a powerful voice inside my chest say, "Son, I love you, too. Come back to Me." I could not speak for a few minutes. I was fighting hard not to cry, but I could not hold the tears back.

For the first time since my childhood, I felt the powerful presence of God. I looked at Junior and said, "Man, I have to go. I don't know how to tell you what just happened to me, but as soon as I can figure it out, I will. One thing I can tell you is that I will never be the same!" He replied, "That's cool, Tom."

I got into my car and said, "Jesus, is that You?" It felt like He sat down beside me and put His arm around me. I wept uncontrollably the whole fifteen-mile drive home. I have never been the same since that glorious morning.

2 Samuel 14:14 says, "For we will surely die and become like water spilled on the ground, which cannot be gathered up again. Yet God does not take away a life; but He devises means, so that His banished ones are not expelled from Him."

The Lord set me up that morning, and I collided into His immeasurable love.

REFOCUS

Friend, wipe the scales of conditional love from your eyes. You and I will never love Him the way He longs to be loved until we believe and embrace the forever enduring love He has for us. We love Him because He first loved us. Lift your eyes and see the One who loves you so much that He preferred death on a cross over spending eternity without you. He absolutely loves you, too, beyond belief. See yourself as the apple of His eye because that is who you are.

"And we have known and believed the love that God has for us. God is love, and he who abides in love abides in God, and God in him" (1 John 4:16).

REKINDLE

Believe the love He has for you, just as you are. Do not worry, He will not leave you the way you are. As you rise and passionately go after Him, He will absolutely set fire to your soul and spirit.

REJOICE

This love relationship is the greatest thing in time and eternity. Today, you are officially one day closer to coming face-to-face with Him. You will look into the eyes of the One who loves you and washed you in His own blood. Rejoice in this unspeakable joy!

REFOCUS

↓

REKINDLE

↓

REJOICE

4

The Promise Of The Greatest Faith

But you, beloved, building yourselves up on your most holy faith, praying in the Holy Spirit. — Jude 1:20

He who speaks in a tongue edifies himself.
— 1 Corinthians 14:4a

Growing up in a Baptist home, I never heard my parents talk negatively about speaking in tongues. However, throughout my childhood, I often heard many different preachers state that it was either "not for today" or "of the devil."

When I came back to Christ at the age of 21 after spending so many years away from Him, I was hungry for more of Him. One day around that time, I was staying at the home of my sister, Kathy, and brother-in-law, Jeff. I was aware that they both prayed in unknown tongues, which they referred to as their "prayer language." They had been talking about speaking in tongues, and it was creating a stirring in my heart.

I slipped into the back bedroom where I was staying, sat on the bed, and told the Lord, "You know that I am a Baptist, or at least that is all I know myself to be, and I have heard people say that speaking in tongues is of the devil. I know Jeff and Kathy are not of the devil, and I don't know two other people who love You more. So, I don't know if You want me to speak in tongues, but if You do, I want it, and I want it now!"

I slapped the bed with my right hand, and when I did, a language that I did not know began to gush out of my mouth. It scared me, and I found it almost impossible to stop speaking in this unknown tongue.

When I finally did stop, I said, "Lord, if I have done something wrong, I am sorry." With that frightened statement, I did not speak in tongues again until a pastor laid his hands on me to receive the baptism of the Holy Spirit a few days later. The very same words came gushing out my mouth again. Pastor Dennis began to jump up and down and shout, "He's got it! He's got it!" From that time on, I began to spend a lot of time praying in this newly found heavenly language.

I could tell you so many amazing things that took place as I prayed in the Spirit, but I will just give you one instance for now.

In 1989, I was working as the Director of Evangelism at Western Michigan Teen Challenge in Muskegon, Michigan. Sam, a staff pastor at WMTC, was over at our home to have dinner with my family and me. We were chatting in the living room while my wife, Tammy, was finishing up the final touches of the meal.

Right in mid-sentence, out of nowhere, I leapt up from the couch and ran as fast I could for the living room stairs. At the same moment I reached the stairs, our 18-month-old daughter, Destiny, was at the top step. She fell forward and landed right into my arms. I shouted praise to God for getting me to the right place at the right time when there was no time for an explanation. If I had not been there in that very moment, my precious daughter could have been severely hurt, or worse.

When I went back to the living room and explained to Sam that I had caught my daughter just in time, he asked me if I had heard her. I told him that I did not hear anything. He asked how I knew to dash to her rescue, and I told him that I did not know how I knew. To this day, I still do not know. But this I do know, when you pray earnestly in the Spirit, miraculous things transpire.

I am a firm believer that the reason why the Apostle Paul walked in such divine revelation was due to his constant connection with Heaven by praying in the unknown tongue (see 2 Corinthians 12:7). Also, in 1 Corinthians 14:18, Paul states that he spoke in tongues more than all. He obviously was not talking about giving messages to the church that were to be interpreted, but rather about his times of private prayer, being alone with God (see 1 Corinthians 14:19). You can blow this off completely and believe that this is not for today, or you can receive this powerful baptism of the Holy Spirit by faith and begin to have your faith explode in blessing after blessing to the world around you.

REFOCUS

Lift your eyes and look unto Jesus, the One who still mightily baptizes the hungry in the Holy Ghost. See Him as the very same yesterday, today, and forever. Praying in the Holy Ghost builds up your most holy faith (Jude 1:20), and speaking in an unknown tongue edifies the speaker (1 Corinthians 14:4), both of which have the same root word. Jude and Paul are speaking of the same thing.

REKINDLE

If you have never received this baptism, begin to pray with all the passion inside you for Jesus to baptize you in the Holy Spirit. If you have, then ask Jesus to immerse you again and even more deeply this time. He loves to answer this kind of prayer.

REJOICE

You say, "Do I have to speak in tongues?" I say, "You get to. Rejoice!" Hungry heart, you are chosen to be a mighty vessel of God, a conduit for the river of the Spirit to flow through to impact many people. Do you receive this word? Then shout, praise, and worship your Almighty Father as an act of faith. Rejoice knowing that He is very pleased with your heart for Him.

5

Jesus Is Exactly Where You Want Him

Draw near to God and He will draw near to you.
Cleanse your hands, you sinners; and purify your hearts,
you double- minded.   — James 4:8

We place the Lord exactly where we want Him, and I have found this to be true in my own life. If you are content with a Jesus that you only talk to on Sundays, you will have a very limited enjoyment of His presence, or none at all.

When I came back to Jesus, I was instantaneously delivered from a seven-year drug and alcohol addiction, without a withdrawal or a regret. However, I made a huge mistake by holding onto my cigarette addiction. I knew of several pastors in my area that grew tobacco to sell, use, or both. That became my benchmark instead of Christ. I am ashamed to tell you that I allowed smoking to keep me at a distance from Jesus for about a year. Jesus put His finger on it, and I was convicted. Yet, I settled with this habit and let it rob me of nearness to Christ. I became so weary from the conviction. I fell on my face one day and cried out to the Lord for help. He heard me, and I was totally delivered from that moment.

Let me give you four "Jesus placement" scenarios.

The atheist: Jesus is so far away that He is not even acknowledged as being in the universe. All atheists will become believers upon being cast into hell. Sadly, however, it will be too late for them to repent. They had no room for God in their thoughts, and God has no room for them in His Heaven. Romans 1:28 says, "And even as they did not like to retain God in their knowledge, God gave them over to a debased mind, to do those things which are not fitting."

The rejecter of Christ: Jesus is a last resort. In a desperate situation, he says "Oh, God, help me!" Jesus is held in the "trunk of their life" so to speak, like some spare tire. Jesus is a total stranger to them, but they will give Him a shot in a crisis. Oh, they believe in a god out there somewhere, but so do all the demons. James 2:19 says, "You believe that there is one God. You do well. Even the demons believe and tremble!"

The backslider: Christ has been known, but now to some degree He has been forgotten. If you have ever been closer to Jesus than you are right now, you have backslidden. This was the case with Christians at the five churches of Ephesus, Sardis, Pergamos, Thyatira and Laodicea.

Revelation 2:4 (Ephesus): you "left your first love."

Revelation 3:1 (Sardis): "you have a name that you

are alive, but you are dead."

Revelation 2:14 (Pergamos): "you have there those who hold the doctrine of Balaam."

Revelation 2:20 (Thyatira): "you allow that woman Jezebel."

Revelation 3:16 (Laodicea): "you are lukewarm."

Five of the seven believing churches were rebuked by the Lord and had a great need for repentance. All five of them had some degree of backsliding in their midst.

Those churches held Jesus at a distance, so to speak. What great similarities with many "believers" today. All five churches were greatly loved of the Lord but sternly threatened by Him. All were called to put Jesus where He belonged. In 1 Peter 3:15, we read, "But sanctify the Lord God in your hearts ..." Sadly, they all had grown content with Christ at a distance.

The disciple: They deny themselves and take up their cross to follow Christ wherever He leads, daily. Luke 14:27 says, "And whoever does not bear his cross and come after Me cannot be My disciple." This one is on fire for God and must have the fuel of Christ's nearness always because he or she is addicted to Jesus. Proverbs 30:15-16, talks about how fire will never say I have had enough. The passage reads:

There are three things that are never satisfied,
Four never say, "Enough!":
The grave,
The barren womb,
The earth that is not satisfied with water —
And the fire never says, "Enough!"

In summary, we put Jesus where we really want Him, and our desire for Jesus is equal to our discipline to be near Him. I have heard it said that a definition of a fanatic is someone who "loves Jesus more than you do." We should make it our aim in life to be able to say that "no one will love Jesus more than I."

REFOCUS

Take a good look at where Jesus is in your life. Is He as near as the air you breathe or do you, like Peter, follow Him from a far?

REKINDLE

Earnestly pray, confess the sin of half-heartedness, wash your hands of sinful habits, and cry out to Jesus for cleansing of sin and double-mindedness.

REJOICE

Hallelujah! He hears your cry. He will answer you with transforming power. You are loved by Him.

6

Angels In Charge

For He shall give His angels charge over you, to keep you in all your ways. — Psalm 91:11

God has put his angels in place as overseers to protect us in all of life's journeys. If this verse were not true, I would not be here to write this little book for you.

When I came back to the Lord, I struggled greatly with accepting the Lord's forgiveness. My sin was exceedingly sinful to say the least. I could not wrap my brain around a love that could forgive one as wicked as I had been. I did not yet place the same value on the blood of Jesus that my Heavenly Father does. Along with my doubts and fears, I was being attacked by the enemy that tested my faith level.

However, in the kindness of my Father, I had a couple

of dramatic encounters with the Angel in charge of me.

One such encounter occurred when I was working at a manufacturing plant, where my department was very loud and noisy. At the time, I was going through an especially tormenting season. I was struggling to find rest in what Jesus had done for me, so much so that one particular night, I was not paying attention to the lane where the electric forklifts were running. I was so preoccupied with the condemnation consuming my thoughts that I stepped out from a blind spot just as a fast-moving forklift that should have taken me out sped by.

I felt a very powerful hand grab me by the right shoulder, and I saw my feet come up off the floor. I was jerked back several feet like a rag doll.

The driver stopped and looked horrified. He shouted, "Are you hurt?" as I turned around to thank whoever it was that had just saved my life. I said, "No, I am fine." "Are you sure?" he asked intently. "I saw you go flying through the air!" I assured him that I had not been hit, and that I was fine.

He shook his head and reluctantly pulled away. While I was standing there totally dumbfounded, I heard the Lord say to my heart, "Fear not, my son, for I am with you." I had a bit of a hallelujah breakdown, and for quite a while after, I was greatly comforted by that experience.

Another encounter I had with supernatural protection was when we moved to Michigan, and I was the lead youth pastor at a church. Even though I had served as a youth pastor for a few years prior to that point, I would still be overcome with waves of guilt from my past. I would get my mind on things that I had committed against

God while backslidden, and be overcome with doubts and fears again and again.

One Saturday morning, I had decided to work on my old car that had a leak in the gas tank, and I had determined to fix it myself. With my bumper jack, I lifted the car up high enough to take the left rear tire off, and crawled up underneath the car. I saw the leak and applied liquid steel to the hole.

My neck was perfectly under the wheel hub when I heard a loud voice call my name. I was startled, so I immediately came out from underneath the car to see who had shouted my name.

In that split second, the car pitched forward, the jack kicked out, and the car came down. The hub was right where my neck had been seconds before. I saw no one to thank for saving my life.

Again, I heard the voice of the Lord say, "Son! I am with you. Do not be faithless, but believe My love, forgiveness, and cleansing of your sin."

REFOCUS

Friend, do you ever struggle with guilt and condemnation from your past? If so, lift your eyes and look closely at that One who said from the cross, "It is finished!" He left nothing undone. God sees that shed blood, and I encourage you to fix your eyes on Jesus, the One who shed His blood for you.

REKINDLE

Lift your voice to the Lord and pray for God to open your eyes to see the finished work of Christ on your behalf.

REJOICE

Believing child of God, your sins are forgiven and for-gotten. He has redeemed you and called you by your name. It is well with your soul. You ought to let out a shout to God with a voice of triumph.

7

Only Believe!

Jesus said to him, "If you can believe, all things are possible to him who believes." — Mark 9:23

But when Jesus heard it, He answered him, saying, "Do not be afraid; only believe, and she will be made well." When He came into the house, He permitted no one to go in except Peter, James, and John, and the father and mother of the girl. — Luke 8:50-51

In my walk with the Lord, the Holy Spirit continues to call out to me about having simple, child-like faith. He causes me to remember the times He has shown His faithfulness and to believe He is still the God of miracles. I can still hear Him say, "Only believe, all things are possible to the one who believes."

Looking back, I am reminded of a time when we were just a young family of three, sitting on the couch watching a Christian television program, circa early 1980s.

Ryan, who is our eldest, was only eighteen months old at the time. He was standing between my wife, Tammy, and me on the couch. Tammy had not been feeling well and said out loud, "My head hurts really bad."

Before I could even reply, Ryan said, "Jeda (Jesus), Momma head!" Instantly, Tammy grabbed her head and said, "It's gone. My head has completely stopped hurting!"

I said, "Son! Pray for me!" Ryan put his little hand on my shoulder and said, "Jeda, Daddy house!"

Just then, the phone rang, and it was my godly, praying, grandmother on the other line. She said to me, "Son, I can't get you off of my mind. I feel that I am supposed to give you $200." No one other than Tammy knew that I still needed $200 to pay the rent.

To my amazement, God proved Himself to be a faithful, miracle-working God in that moment. Although this was many years ago, God has continued to work miracles all throughout my life.

Fast forward not so many years ago. Our church was going through a very difficult time financially. It was bad, to say the least. I felt so responsible because it appeared that I had led my church into biting off more than we could chew. But ... God!

I was crying out to God one day during that difficult time and said to Him, "Lord, if I had the money to pay all these bills, I would pay them myself. You know I would. But I can't!" His voice interrupted my moaning and groaning, and He said, "Can you believe?" It was like a slap in the face.

In response, I said, "Yes!" Just then, I raised up and

looked over the top of the couch where I was kneeling to look up and see a sign in the window that said, "BELIEVE." "Okay, Lord, I hear You," I replied.

One Wednesday evening in the following days after crying out to God for our church's finances, I arrived at our church service and was met by my wife, Tammy, in the back of the sanctuary. Tammy discreetly said, "I have something to tell you after the service." "Is it bad?" I asked. She said, "No, it's not bad."

I was so distracted by what she needed to tell me that I could hardly teach. As soon as I finished, I went to her and said, "What was it that you wanted to tell me?"

She said, "This afternoon, someone dropped off a check for $15,000!" I began to chant, "I believe, I believe, I believe, I believe, I believe, I believe, I do, I do, I do, I do! I really do!"

Friend, let me tell you that if you stand believing on God's promises, and do not let go, Heaven will come through for you. Be glad that it does not depend on your goodness or your faithfulness. It depends on His.

REFOCUS

Lift your eyes away from your goodness and your faithfulness. That never aids our faith. Look away from the mountain of impossibility. Lift your eyes high above that mountain and see Jesus, the faithful, true, and Almighty One as He comes to the aid of all who call on His name!

REKINDLE

Now fervently pray, believing. Know that He hears you, and He will show you great and mighty things that you do not even know.

REJOICE

He has made everything beautiful in its time (Ecclesiastes 3:11). ALL THINGS ARE POSSIBLE, ONLY BELIEVE! If you believe Him, rejoice in Him.

8

God Will Always Pay His Laborers

Who ever goes to war at his own expense? Who plants a vineyard and does not eat of its fruit? Or who tends a flock and does not drink of the milk of the flock?
— 1 Corinthians 9:7

In the winter of 1986, Tammy and I loaded everything we could either in or on top of our 1972 Olds Vista Cruiser station wagon. We left our family, church, and friends behind in the beautiful mountains of Burnsville, North Carolina, and headed north to Saginaw County, Michigan.

Ryan was three and a half years old, and Tammy was pregnant with our second child, Sarah. We had a job, but unfortunately, there was no pay. The mission was to be the youth pastor at Burt Assembly of God in Burt, Michigan. The late Reverend Steve Hammond had been my pastor in North Carolina, and then later, he took the pastorate position at the church in Burt. A few months later, he invited me to come join him.

The Church took a step of faith and rented a place for our family about a quarter of a mile from the church property. I took a job working in a machine shop for a man in our church. I averaged making around $100 a week, and someone, anonymously and faithfully, gave us $40 a week. So the rent was paid, and we were bringing in about $560 a month total. The Lord took care of us and met all of our needs during that year.

The Lord started moving among the youth in our church, and many were coming to Jesus and catching on fire for God. We were so happy and blessed with our new church family. They were some of the most wonderful people that I have ever known. I began to feel such a stir to go into full-time ministry. I could not shake it. What was I supposed to do, quit my job and take care of my family on a $40-a-week offering? Finally, early one morning at work around 3 a.m., all alone in the shop, I told the Lord if he wanted me to become a full-time youth pastor, I was willing, but I had to know that it was Him calling me.

A few days later, I went to serve as a youth camp counselor at FaHoLo in Grass Lake, Michigan. God moved so powerfully at that camp, and we counselors were burning the candle at both ends. I was blessed to have a little cabin to myself.

One night after midnight, I came in and collapsed on my bed totally exhausted. With a wake-up time of 5 a.m., I was hoping to get four hours of sleep. The presence of the Lord came into that cabin so strong that sleep fled from me. I got out of the bed and knelt down. I asked, "What is it, Lord?" Total silence. In a few minutes, I crawled back into bed. I was wide awake. I knew the Lord wanted to say something to me, but I heard nothing.

Again, I got out of bed and knelt beside it. I prayed, "Lord, please, I must get some sleep." Nothing. A bit frustrated, I got back into bed and said, "Lord, I am going to sleep. You can give me a dream or something. I have to get some rest." But instead of going to sleep, I became more and more awake.

It must have been after 3 a.m. when He finally spoke. I heard an audible, loud whisper, "Quit your job." I sat up in bed and said, "What? There is no way we can make it on $40 a week!"

Then He spoke again, but inside my heart this time, "Do you trust Me?" I said, "Of course, I trust You. Haven't I proven that?" Again, He spoke, saying, "Go home and give Les (my boss) a two-week notice." I told Him that I would, but He would have to figure out a way to take care of my family. Well, He already had.

For weeks I had been having visions of pastoring the church. I kept rebuking them, but they kept coming. I thought that I must have had some sort of a character defect. Maybe deep down I did want to pastor the church, but I really did not think that I did.

We scraped up enough money to go back to see our family and church in North Carolina for a few days. As I walked into the church building, a young man who had worked for me before was sitting on the back pew. His name was Kenny. He smiled at me and said, "The Lord wants me to ask you a question." I said, "What is it,

Kenny?" Kenny said, "Tom, Timothy did not always stay with the Apostle Paul, did he? Do you know what I am talking about?"

I knew right then that God was calling me to be pastor at Burt Assembly of God, but I did not know how I was going to break it to Pastor Steve. I was praying, "How on earth will this transition take place? Steve is my dearest friend in the world."

One day, he came to my office and said very directly that I needed to come to his office because he had something he needed to talk to me about. So I followed him back to his office, thinking that I must have done something wrong because of the seriousness of his countenance.

Steve sat down behind his desk and said, "Tom, I have been hoping you would come talk to me, but I guess I am going to have to talk to you. God is calling me to leave this church, and I believe He is calling you to become the pastor."

With a nervous laugh, I said, "Pastor, I know nothing about being a senior pastor. I am sure that they will not want me." He said, "Well, I have already talked to the Board about it, and they are very excited at the thought of it."

I was stunned, and we prayed for the will of the Lord to be done.

A few weeks later, there was a special business meeting, and I was elected as senior pastor with a 100 percent vote. A few days following, we moved from our little trailer to a beautiful, four bedroom home beside the church. The day we moved out of the trailer, the new owners were moving in, and we moved into the parsonage.

We were salaried far more than I had ever made. God is mind-blowing when you let go and let God be God.

REFOCUS

You and I both know that God is far, far greater than we can fathom, right? Lift your eyes and see Him as the Master of your life who does all things well.

REKINDLE

Take a moment and let your faith rise. Make a declaration to trust Him like never before, and ask Him to help you build a bonfire of God-pleasing faith in your soul. Expect Him to do it.

REJOICE

Let your faith-filled praises ring out loud. Faithful is He who has called you, and He will do it. God is about to catapult you into a whole new realm of miracles. If you believe it, rejoice with all your heart.

REFOCUS

↓

REKINDLE

↓

REJOICE

9

Who Is Helen?

The Lord God has given Me the tongue of the learned, that I should know how to speak a word in season to him who is weary. He awakens Me morning by morning, He awakens My ear to hear as the learned.
— Isaiah 50:4

I n the same church that was mentioned in Chapter 8, I later became the senior pastor. My youth pastor, George, loved to go out with me to witness to people as we served in the ministry together.

One particular day of sharing the love of Jesus on the streets, we noticed a young man who stuck his thumb out while we were driving toward town. George and I just laughed and said, "There's one!" We stopped, and the man on the road got in the backseat seemingly grateful for a ride. While we were introducing ourselves and making small talk, the Holy Spirit told me to ask him, "Who is Helen?" I looked back at him in the rear-view mirror, asked if he knew who she was, and his countenance quickly changed. He scowled and said, "She is the biggest hypocrite in the world! She says she's a Christian. Ha! If that is what a Christian is, I want nothing to do with Christianity!"

With a look of surprise on his face, he then asked, "Why did you ask me about Helen? Do you know her or something?" "No," I replied. "I just felt that the Lord wanted me to ask if you knew her." He was visibly shaken. "The Lord told you that?" he questioned. "Why would He tell you that?"

I began to explain to him that I believed the Lord had revealed her name to me because I felt that the Lord was saying Helen had been a stumblingblock to him and was keeping him from seeing the Lord, who wanted to save him.

George and I told him of God's great salvation and His love for him. We asked if he wanted to know Jesus and have Him become his Lord and Savior, and he excitedly responded, "Yes!" We prayed with him, encouraged him in the Lord, and he told us he would find a church to attend. While we never saw him again, we knew that God had given us a divine appointment that day.

Friend, I have shared this with you to encourage you to be available to the Holy Spirit. I could tell you of so many testimonies of divine appointments through the course of my life. I only recount this to emphasize the truth that Jesus came to seek and to save those who are lost. He wants to work with you in this regard. He will speak things to you about people that He alone knows.

He does this so they will know that He cares for them and wants to be Lord and Savior of their lives.

REFOCUS

Turn your eyes on the great Shepherd and Bishop of our souls. Let Him give you a word of knowledge for a lost or backslidden person.

REKINDLE

Pray now in earnest that He will give you a new burden for souls. Let him give you an ear to hear and a mouth to speak His life-giving message to others.

REJOICE

He absolutely will. How do I know? Because He has called you and ordained you to go and bring forth fruit. If you receive it, shout praises to God.

REFOCUS

↓

REKINDLE

↓

REJOICE

10

Wonder-Working Power Of God

*And these signs will follow those who believe; they will lay
hands on the sick, and they will recover.*

— Mark 16:17(a)-18(b)

While at the first church I pastored, Burt Assembly
of God in Michigan, my colleague, the late
Reverend Roosevelt Hunter, and I were praying
for people at one of our church services. A lady in our
church suffered from extreme scoliosis of the spine and
had come forward for prayer. When we anointed her
with oil, laid hands on her, and began to pray, we felt a
tremendous popping in her back. She began to weep and
shout because she knew that Jesus had touched her.

Later that evening, Kelly, her twelve-year-old daughter,
called me crying. I asked her what was wrong. Kelly
explained that her mother had told her to look at her

spine. When Kelly saw her mother's spine, she was over-whelmed with joy because of what the Lord had done. Her mother's spine was completely normal; it was straight as an arrow. All praise to the Great Physician.

On another occasion, at the same church, a woman came to one of our night services. This was her first time visiting our church. She asked us to pray for her brother who was in a hospital in California. She told us that he suffered with inoperable cancer in his brain and had been given only hours to live. She was flying the next morning to, hopefully, see him one last time. In that moment, I felt directed by the Holy Spirit to anoint a handkerchief and pray over it. I called the leaders to come up and pray for this man as we collectively laid our hands on the cloth. I gave it to her and told her to lay it on his body when she saw him. She agreed that she would.

Some weeks later, the lady attended our church again and asked if she could give a testimony. I said, "Certainly." The dear woman told us that when she arrived at her brother's bedside, he was in a coma. The nurse said he would never make it through the night. The cancer was all over his body, and he was shutting down. The woman laid the handkerchief on her dying brother. She turned to the nurse and asked her to call her room if anything changed in the night.

The nurse called her in the early hours of the next morning. The lady asked her if her brother was gone, and the nurse said, "No, but he is going to be." The woman replied, "I will come right over!" The nurse said, "Yes, please do. Your brother is up, asking where he can find his pants, and what would he have to do to get something to eat around this place." He had not eaten anything by mouth in days. The hospital ran numerous scans and tests. They could not find any trace of cancer in the man's body.

You should have heard our church shouting and praising God when this lady told the testimony of her brother's supernatural healing. In the past three decades, we have been eye witnesses to countless healings, and we believe the best is still yet to come!

REFOCUS

Oh, friend, lift your eyes to the marvelous Healer, Jesus Christ. See Him touching sick bodies and doing the impossible.

REKINDLE

Intensely pray that He will make you one of those believers who lays hands on the sick, watches them recover, and brings great glory to the name of Jesus.

REJOICE

Lift high praise to the Lord knowing that He has heard you and will send you out into the harvest with healing, signs, and wonders in His name. Worship Him most of all because He has written your name in the Lamb's book of life.

REFOCUS

↓

REKINDLE

↓

REJOICE

11

God's Got Your Number

A man's heart plans his way, but the Lord directs his way.
his steps.   — Proverbs 16:9

While pastoring my first church in Michigan, I began to feel restless. My wife and I loved the people dearly, but I had an itch to plant an inner city church. The Michigan District of the Assemblies of God was working hard to plant churches in the state, especially in the more unreached areas. Two of my dear minister friends, Tim Dilena and Roosevelt Hunter, had planted a church in Highland Park (Detroit), Michigan. I had been there numerous times, and I was so excited about planting a church in the nearby Brightmoor area.

Our plan was to be a part of Revival Tabernacle and sit under their ministry for six months, then launch out from there to plant a church of our own. It was in an extremely rough area, and the "hero" in me wanted to charge the place with Gospel-guns blazing. The District heard my heart and gave consent for me to proceed with the initial steps to be an inner city church planter. I was so excited.

While all this was in process, I was helping another pastor friend, Doug Hammond, with his youth ministry two hours away in Olivet, Michigan. I was about to leave for Olivet one Wednesday afternoon, and before heading out, I handed the church planter application to Tammy. It was time for her to fill out her portion of the application. In a few minutes, she handed it back to me. I quickly scanned her responses. One of the questions read, "Which answer best describes how you feel about being a church planter's wife: 1) Very eager, 2) Eager, 3) Submissive, 4) Reluctant, 5) Very reluctant.

Tammy had not answered this particular question. I asked her which one best described how she felt. She answered confidently, "Submissive." I said, "Honey, that's sweet, but it's not good enough." She said, "Tom, I am sorry, but that is the best I can do." I thought, "There is something wrong here, and I have to find out what it is."

With great frustration, I walked into the bathroom and shut the door. I told the Lord I knew that He had called us to leave Burt, Michigan, and reminded Him we had only two more weeks before we had to go. I told the Lord how I really wanted to start a church in Brightmoor. I went on to tell Him that if He did not want us to go there, I was willing to pastor an existing church, but I had one condition. I said to Him, "I am not going to send out any resumes. If You have a church somewhere else for me to pastor, You know my phone number."

Within the hour, the phone rang. Tammy took the call, and she was so excited. I thought it was Rosalie, a dear intercessor friend of ours who lived in Detroit. She must have found a house for us, and now Tammy is getting excited about going to Detroit, I thought.

I could hardly wait for her to get off the phone. I only had a few minutes to talk until I needed to leave for Olivet youth ministry.

As soon as she hung up, I said, "Was that Rosalie?" "No. You will never guess who that was," she replied. I asked, feeling curious, "Who was it?" She said, "That was Carol Baker." I had not heard from Carol in years. I asked Tammy what she wanted, and she said, "Carol has been praying for nine months for a new pastor because the interim is about to resign. She has been hearing our names all this time, and today she got our phone number from our former pastor. She told the Lord if we were able to come, then she knew the Lord had been telling her that we were the ones for the job."

Carol did not even know that I was in the ministry. You would think I would have been elated, but I was not. No, to the contrary, I was completely deflated.

During the two-hour drive to the church in Olivet, I told the Lord that I did not want to go to some wide place in the road. I wanted to go to the inner city. He said nothing to me. I spoke to those young people that night with sub-zero anointing.

On the trip home, the Lord began to straighten me out. He let me know, in so many words, that I was the clay, and He was the potter. If He wanted me to go to Antarctica, then I had better purchase a parka. And do not forget how I had told Him earlier that He knew my phone number. By the time I got home, I was willing to be obedient to his voice, so much so, I was even ready to clean the toilets of that church.

On numerous occasions during my 30-day resignation period, several different people approached me stating that God had given them a verse for me: Zechariah 4:6. A well-known verse that says, "Not by might, not by power, but by my Spirit says the Lord."

On that Sunday morning in June of 1991, I was in the pastor's office at Batesville Assembly of God in Batesville, Indiana, the church where Carol Baker was praying for a new pastor. I told the Lord that it seemed so obvious that He had called me to pastor the church, but I wanted it in writing. I wanted His word on it because He had always confirmed our steps with His Word.

He spoke to my heart and said, "Open the top left drawer of the pastor's desk." The drawer had only one item in it. It was the church letterhead. Across the top of the letterhead it read: "Not by might, not by power, but by my Spirit says the Lord."

I bowed my head and said, "I'm sorry, Lord, for arguing with You. Please have Your way today." The church elected me with a 98 percent vote that morning. We happily served there for exactly three years.

REFOCUS

To carry out the will of God, we have to look away from our own agenda and look unto Jesus. We must submit our plans to the Lord and be willing for Him to lead us any way He desires to lead us.

REKINDLE

To "delight yourself in the Lord" simply means to be easily influenced and persuaded by the Lord. It is kind of like being able to talk an intoxicated person into just about anything. Ask the Lord to fill you so full of His Spirit that you would be joyfully willing to follow Him anywhere.

REJOICE

The plans the Lord has for you are far, far greater than the greatest plan you can design for yourself. Thank Him that He knows "your number," and tell Him you are expecting a call from Heaven that will bring further glory and honor to His name. Praise Him while you expectantly wait on Him. Go ahead and shout. God always returns His calls.

REFOCUS

↓

REKINDLE

↓

REJOICE

12

God Is Not An Austere Taskmaster

*He will feed His flock like a shepherd; He will gather
the lambs with His arm, and carry them in His bosom,
and gently lead those who are with young.*
                                                    — Isaiah 40:11

Our move to Batesville, Indiana, was undeniably God's idea, but it was a sizable cut in pay from our former church in Burt, Michigan. Almost immediately, the pressure was on.

Early one Saturday morning, I was on my knees praying for provision for the bills I had spread out in front of me. I said to the Lord, "We do not have enough money to pay all these bills. What am I to do, Father?" I heard Him as clearly as I have ever heard His voice say, "Take your family to the zoo today." I laughed and replied, "That is not what I am praying about, Lord." He firmly repeated,

"Take your family to the zoo today." I said, "Tammy will never go for this." He said, "Tell her I told you to go to the zoo today."

Rather than debate with the Lord any further, I told her that we were taking the kids to the zoo. She asked me how it was right to take the little money we had to pay toward our bills and go to the zoo. I said, "All I know is the Lord told me to do it." With that, she reluctantly consented.

I also added, "We are going to the Cincinnati Zoo." The Lord spoke to my heart and said, "No, you are going to the Indianapolis Zoo." I told the family there was a change in plans, and we were going to the Indianapolis Zoo instead. Our kids were surprised; well, except for Tyler. He was just a baby at the time.

When we arrived, there was a long line of people at the entrance waiting for the zoo to open. I remember standing there thinking, "I must be crazy. How is this being responsible, taking the bill money to go to the zoo for entertainment? We just need to be strong and endure the financial squeeze."

I noticed a lady waving her hand maybe fifty feet ahead of us in line. She was looking right at me. When she realized that she had caught my attention, she said, "Sir, would you like some tickets?" I looked all around to see who she was talking to. I looked back, and she said, "Yes! You, Sir!" I was in disbelief.

There were people much closer to her, and she was offering tickets to us. "I have six tickets!" she exclaimed. I rushed up to her, and asked if she was sure, and she told me that she wanted us to have them. I thanked her over and over again, and she just kept telling me that I was welcome.

I wish you could have seen the look on Tammy's and my children's faces when I returned with the free, not cheap, tickets in my hand. It was like a miracle. We were in the right place, at the right time, with one extremely kind lady. I was overwhelmed. I did not know whether to laugh or to cry.

While we were still flipping out over the goodness of God, the lady started calling out to me again. She was waving for me to come back. My heart sank. "Oh, no. She has changed her mind," I thought. So, I made my way back to her, and she said, "Sir, I am so sorry, but I forgot to give you the six meal tickets, too." I nearly burst into tears.

Needless to say, it was an unforgettable day in our family's history. The Lord wanted to bless my family, and bless us He did. The money set aside for our bills remained intact.

REFOCUS

In John 10:4, the Bible tells us that Jesus, the Good Shepherd, goes before His sheep. Look to Him. He is leading you to green pastures and still waters. He is always preparing a table for you, right in the devil's face. Whatever difficulty you might be facing at this time, just see the One who never takes His eyes off of you. Know that He wants you to have times of refreshing. He is not some hard-nosed boss demanding that you work, work, work. He has unforgettable adventures for you and your family.

REKINDLE

Let your faith in His faithfulness rise in your heart. Begin to pray fervently to Him who knows no limitation. Stir up your memories of the times Jesus has come through for you, right on time.

REJOICE

Begin to shout unto God with a voice of triumph. Praise Him for His countless interventions on your behalf. Worship Him because He is worthy, knowing that another testimony is in the making. HALLELUJAH!

13

The All-Supplying God

*Indeed I have all and abound. I am full, having received
from Epaphroditus the things sent from you, a sweet-
smelling aroma, an acceptable sacrifice, well pleasing
to God. And my God shall supply all your need accord-
ing to His riches in glory by Christ Jesus.*
— Philippians 4:18-19

I have noticed through the years that Christians love
to claim the portion of the verse in Philippians that
says: "God shall supply all your need." I am confident
that if people are sacrificial in their giving to the work of
the Lord, they can absolutely stand on this promise and
expect supernatural supply.

However, I am not so confident that the self-centered
believer should expect too much. Please do not take this
and think that my intention is to blow my own horn in

what I am about to say. I only want to encourage you to dare to give until it hurts.

In the early 1990s, I made two trips to Romania. I was absolutely amazed with the faith and passion of The Good Samaritan Church of Ocna Mures, in Transylvania. Pastor Nico and his dear family would walk eight miles round-trip to their church. My friend, Roger, and I were moved to invite our church board to dig into our pockets and come up with enough money to purchase a van for the Gatea family. Thankfully, money was given toward this need.

In my heart, I wanted to give something significant, but I did not have the funds. I prayed and asked the Lord to tell me what to give toward the van. I heard Him say, "Give $500." I said, "Lord, you know I don't have that much money to give." I suggested giving $200. But I heard Him say it again, "$500."

"I cannot give $500, Lord!" He responded by telling me to put it on my credit card, but I told him that I just could not do that. Then He said to me, "You have done it for yourself." With that, I made my way to the bank to get $500 on my credit card to help purchase the van.

Some years later, I was pastoring a church in Nashville, Tennessee. A dear couple, Mae and Stan, from our church in Batesville, Indiana, had come for a visit. We were praying in the sanctuary with them when, suddenly, Mae looked at me and said, "Don't you buy a car! The Lord is going to give you one." I told her that I would not buy a car, but I would wait for the one the Lord would supply.

She did not know that I had been praying for a car. We were praying about launching a Teen Challenge back in Indiana, and I knew that I would have to drive throughout the area raising funds for the ministry. I could not wear out our vehicle and leave my family without transportation.

A few weeks later, I was more confident of the call to go back and pioneer a Teen Challenge center. We came home from our son's tee-ball game one night, and there was a like-new, Pontiac Sunbird parked in our driveway. I recognized the car from our church, but we did not see the couple who owned the vehicle. We concluded that they must have gone for a walk when they did not find us at home.

Then it hit me, they left the car because they were giving it to us. Tammy said there must be another explanation. Within a few minutes, they drove up in their other car. It seemed strange, but we invited them in. They visited for a few moments, and then Dixie stood to his feet and said, "Well we came in two cars, and we are leaving in one." He extended his hand and gave me the folded-up title and the keys. They told us that the Lord had told them to give us their car.

A few days later, Dixie came to my office. He apologized and said, "How rude of me, I gave you a car and did not give you a tag. He handed me the money and left me sitting there in thankful awe and wonder.

I went to the tag office and made the purchase. When I went out to the car to put the tag on, I was stunned. The tag read: "TLC" with three numbers that followed. Some months before, my dear friend, Dave Tennant from Michigan, had emailed me saying the Lord says that He is going to take care of the Anglins with "TLC"! I put another

150,000 miles on that wonderful car for Teen Challenge.

Several years later, we had four drivers in our family and only two cars. It was a dilemma with our busy schedules. One Saturday morning, while Tammy and I were having some coffee, I told Tammy we needed another car.

She agreed, but stated that we had no money for a car. I replied, "Well, the Lord can provide, can He not?" She agreed, and with that, we prayed together believing the Lord would provide.

Within minutes the phone rang. Pastor J. Calaway asked me if we were going be home for a little while. I told him sure and to come on over. Tammy said, "What do you think they are coming over for?" I said, "I believe they are going to give us a car!" She asked me if I had talked to them about our need. I told her that I had not. A short while later, they drove up in two vehicles. I knew then that God had heard our prayer. They visited briefly and told us they had to go, but they were leaving their minivan with us.

One night, our daughter was driving home from work and crashed the minivan. It messed up the entire right side. Thankfully, no one was hurt, but the entire right side of the van was messed up. It was driveable, but cosmetically, it did not look great.

Soon after the wreck, we invited Dr. Michael L. Brown to come minister at our church. I told the Lord I did not want to be prideful, but I really did not want to chauffeur our special guest in our van looking as it did.

One afternoon just a few days later, the phone rang. It was my dear friend, David. He and his wife had gone to Romania with me. David asked me if they could come over to eat pizza that night. I told him, "Sure!" When I hung up the phone, I said to Tammy, "Pizza and a car!"

I then told her that David and his wife were coming over for pizza, and that I was pretty sure they were going to give us a car. Tammy said, "Why would you think that?" I told her that I had prayed asking God for a better car. Well, you guessed it. We ate pizza together, and they left us that night with a title, keys, and a beautiful silver Mitsubishi Montero Sport SUV.

Oh, and one more thing. In 1982, I was directed by the Lord to sell my beloved 250 Bultaco trials bike and give the money to the church where I served as youth pastor to help pay off some bills. Guess what! Just a few years ago, Mark, a man in my church, restored a "1982" 650 street bike and just gave it to me. It is worth far more than that old dirt bike! Yep, I'll say it again, "You cannot outgive God!"

REFOCUS

Look unto Jesus and see Him again as the God you will never, ever outgive!

REKINDLE

Pray and ask Him to stir you up about living a more sacrificial lifestyle. Pray and expect the Lord to show you what to sow into His Kingdom's work.

REJOICE

He has heard you! Praise Him, and believe Him to direct you into what He wants to bless! Hallelujah, He will!

REFOCUS

↓

REKINDLE

↓

REJOICE

14

So How Does That Work?

O our God, will You not judge them? For we have no power against this great multitude that is coming against us; nor do we know what to do, but our eyes are upon You.
— 2 Chronicles 20:12

In the summer of 1998, I was lying on the floor, face-down, in my office in Nashville, Tennessee. I was crying out to God because I was feeling a release from the church I had only pastored for a year. We loved the people greatly, and it was apparent that they loved us. Yet, I knew the Lord was dealing with me to trust Him and to let it go.

I asked Him to speak clearly about this tear in my soul. Then I heard His voice say, "Go to your desk, pick up your pen, write, and you will know my answer."

I stood up from the floor, wiped the tears from my

eyes, and sat down at my desk. I picked up my pen and put it to paper.

With absolutely no idea what I would write, this is what I heard Him say:

"My son, I am calling your name. I see your tears, I know your pain. I love you with an everlasting love. A love without clouds awaits you above. I need you to search in My stead for the lost. Are you still willing, and have you counted the cost? If you are now ready to run for the prize, to cast out the devil, and open blind eyes, hear what I am saying. I am saying to go. Do not ever doubt that I have called you to show that I am still a God Who cares for fallen man. Now, go in My Name, and I will unfold My plan."

In awe, I sat and wept some more, knowing that I had my answer. However, I had no idea how I would move to an unknown destination and take care of a family of six.

Some time later, an invitation came from one of my successors in a church that I had pastored in Batesville, Indiana. He asked me to consider being on their church staff acting in the role of an evangelist. There was no money involved, but it was a gracious offer from an incredible pastor. It was also a place to hang my hat with dear friends who loved us. We prayerfully accepted the offer. With no income to pay bills, we stepped out. We rolled into town with our car and a very large moving truck with no place to unload it. My kids were asking me, "Where are we going to live, Dad?" I simply replied, "Our Father knows!"

I had been praying intensely in the Spirit one morning, and I saw a house in my mind's eye in an "old money" neighborhood that looked like a home I had always admired in town. It had been built way back by a man named Romweber whose company had built furniture for the White House. I drove into the neighborhood, and my kids were asking jokingly, "Are we going to live with the old, rich people, Dad?" We all laughed until I drove up in front of the house that I had seen. There in the front yard was a sign that said, "FOR RENT." It was beautiful, but to live there seemed to be a farfetched idea. I thought it would rent for a fortune in a Fortune-500 town. What would it hurt to inquire though?

I called the number on the sign the next day. The house had recently been purchased by a very successful attorney. I learned later that he was an agnostic. With the prompting of the Holy Spirit, I asked him what it would rent for. He told me since it needed some updates, he would rent it for $600 a month. Well, it might as well have been $6,000 a month given our financial situation, but with faith, I said, "We would like to rent the house." He asked me what I did for a living. I told him that I was an evangelist. As he rolled his eyes at me, he asked, "How does that work? Are you like Billy Graham?" I laughed out loud and said, "Hardly!" He asked me how I intended to pay my rent and continued to tell me that he expected the rent to, always, be on time.

I said, "Well, wherever I preach, they will give me an honorarium, and besides that, my Father is extremely wealthy, and He will back me up whenever I need Him to!" He gave me that "well, why didn't you say so" look, shook my hand, and agreed to rent us the house. After he walked away, I asked the Lord to never let us be a day late on the rent because I knew it would give him even more cause to reject a personal God.

Shortly after we had moved in, all of our money was gone. I took a job as a welder at the casket factory in town. There was still not enough to cover all of our bills. I cried out to the Lord, "Father, please tell me what to do!" I instantly heard Him say, "Write the check." I gasped for breath and said, "I don't have the money to cover the check." He said, "Do you not think I am good for it? Remember, I will back you up."

With that, I told Tammy to write the check. She looked at me as though I had lost my mind and said, "Did God tell you to do that?" I told her that I was certain He had. She let me know that I needed to be sure that God had told me to do this because writing a bad check is a crime. We prayed and put the check in the mail.

The next day, Tammy came to me with three brand new one hundred-dollar bills in her hand. Her eyes were as big as saucers. I said, "Girl, have you been holding out on me?" Tammy said, "No! I found them in my purse, and I promise I do not know how they got in there!" I told her, "That's fantastic, but we are only halfway there."

The very next day an envelope came in the mail with no return address and no note inside. The only contents in the envelope were three brand new one hundred-dollar bills. The envelope was postmarked Baltimore, Maryland. We did not know anyone from Baltimore. To this day, it is a mystery to us how the Lord provided the money to us just in time. We ran to the bank and deposited the $600, and the check was good!

REFOCUS

Beloved reader, our Heavenly Father has truly got our backs! Take another look at the book of Acts. He was Savior, Deliverer, Healer, Provider, Miracle-worker, Counselor, Comforter, Protector, and Friend. He is no different for us today. See Him again as the One who compels you to cast your every care on Him!

REKINDLE

Trust in Him at all times, you people; Pour out your heart before Him: God is a refuge for us. Selah (Psalm 62:8). Yes, pour out your burden and your request with high praises, believing that He has heard you!

REJOICE

He has heard you, and He will answer right on time, every time! HALLELUJAH!

REFOCUS

↓

REKINDLE

↓

REJOICE

15

Do You Believe God's Timing Is Perfect?

Trust in the Lord with all your heart, and lean not on your own understanding; in all your ways acknowledge Him, and He shall direct your paths. — Proverbs 3:5-6

My family and I were so sad the day that I had to put down our fourteen-year-old dog, Lolly. We loved our sweet English springer spaniel so much! That same day, the Lord gave me a heart-wrenching open vision.

I arrived at the veterinarian's office with Lolly and struggled to get her out of the car. I was trying to be strong because she was sick and suffering, but I was an emotional wreck, knowing that I had to take her in to be put to sleep. A lady that worked at the veterinarian clinic came up beside me and said, "Mr. Anglin, please let me take her. You don't need to go in. She is going to go to sleep and have no more suffering." I said goodbye to Lolly, and the nice lady carried her into the building. Lolly turned her head and looked back at me as if to ask, "Aren't you coming?"

In that moment, out of nowhere, I went into an open vision. I saw dozens of little, dark-skinned children foraging through a mountain of garbage searching for anything they could find to eat.

I asked the Lord, "Who are these little children?" He answered me and said, "Tom, you loved your old dog. You love your family, church family, and the people around you. But I love these helpless little ones. They represent millions of starving children all over the world, and there are not enough people who care deeply enough to help them."

When the Lord said that to me, I experienced a level of sorrow that I have never known, even to this day. The pain in my heart was almost unbearable.

Once I got back home, I sat on my bed and began to sob. I could not control it, and I felt like I could die. Tammy came into the bedroom and began to console me. She thought I was grieving over Lolly. I was crying so much that I could not speak to her.

She began to tell me that everything was going to be alright and that I was the only one in the family who could have taken Lolly. She was suffering so much, and it had to be done. When I could finally speak, I told her that I was not crying over Lolly but was so emotional because of the vision I just had. We held each other as I told her what I had seen.

The next morning, a lady in our church called me. She was excited to tell me that she was going on a mission trip. I asked her, "What kind of mission is it?" She said, "We are going to a very poor village in Mexico. We will be taking food to little children who have to dig through garbage to find something to eat."

I nearly lost it again! I told her about the vision that I had experienced the night before, and she was speechless. I shared the verse that the Lord had given to me after the vision, which was Lamentations 4:4. The verse states: "The tongue of the infant clings to the roof of its mouth for thirst; the young children ask for bread, but no one breaks it for them." She told me that was the very same verse the pastor, who was also going on the mission trip, gave their team. Now, we were both speechless.

Prior to having this vision, I had resigned the church I was pastoring in Lufkin, Texas. We loved our dear church family in Lufkin, but we were like a square peg in a round hole. My plans after resigning were to launch a ministry that targeted the poor and addicted. We were going to stay in the area and establish the ministry in Lufkin, but we would need to move to a new home and find a new source of income. The Lord miraculously opened a door for us to move to a beautiful home across town. It was the kind of home that I had always dreamed that I could provide for my family. It was not cheap, but somehow, I knew the Lord wanted us to be in that home.

This was in 2005, and Florida had been devastated by four major hurricanes during the previous year. An evangelist friend of mine invited me to go with him to Florida and take a job working in disaster relief. I agreed to the job for the purpose of having an income. I was able to purchase an old dump truck to join the relief forces, and it was in this particular job that I learned how it felt to be homeless. There was not a hotel room available within a one-hundred-mile radius, so I slept in my dump truck and showered at truck stops.

Despite this, I was at least able to make some money to send to my family at home. It was a difficult season, and I missed them more than I had ever dreamed I could. The time spent away from my family, working this job, produced in my heart a determination to start a ministry for the homeless, broken, and addicted.

After weeks of work there, I got a chance to go home for a few days. I was mowing our massive lawn and praying about our situation when I heard the Lord ask me if I was willing to go anywhere He wanted me to go. I said, "Of course, I am, Lord!" He said, "Even going back to Hammond, Indiana?" I carefully thought about it and said, "Yes, Lord, even to Hammond, Indiana." He said, "Do you believe my timing is perfect?"

I told Him that I certainly did believe that. He said, "Ask Tammy if she is willing to go anywhere, even back to Hammond, Indiana, and if she believes My timing is perfect?"

I went to Tammy and asked. She responded with, "Yes, of course," to all three questions.

Within an hour after I finished mowing the lawn, our phone rang. It was Pastor J. Calaway from Hammond, Indiana. He asked me if I would pray about coming back to Hammond. I was floored! He had no idea that the Lord had just asked me if I was willing to go back. We began to pray intensely and realized there was a big problem. We had signed an eighteen-month lease for our home, or so we thought. We had been living there only five months. I retrieved the lease agreement and, to my surprise, it was a six-month lease, which we confirmed with our landlord.

Tammy and I began to pray, "Lord, if you want us to go back to Hammond, then we are going to need at least $10,000 by the end of February." That was just a month away. The most money we were ever able to generate was a little over $2,000 in a month. A few days after we prayed for $10,000, the Lord spoke to my heart and said, "I am going to give you more than you asked for because you did not ask for enough."

God supernaturally supplied us with over $13,000 right on time that month! It was enough money to pay all our bills, to help us move, and to live on for a few weeks until we could get established. His will and His timing are always perfect!

REFOCUS

Friend, what impossible situation are you up against? If you do not need this now, you may need this for future reference. Look away from what appears to be insurmountable, and look into the eyes of the Almighty Mountain-mover.

REKINDLE

Begin to pray with a trusting heart. Cry out to Him to fill you with new faith and obedience to do exactly what He is asking of you. Let the Holy Spirit build a fire of willingness inside of you.

REJOICE

Sometimes, you just need to let your hair down and praise God with shouting and dancing like David did. The Lord has something wonderful in the making, and He will not disappoint your faith!

16

When The Light Goes Out

*But when I looked for good, evil came to me; and when
I waited for light, then came darkness.* — Job 30:26

*Who among you fears the Lord? Who obeys the voice of
His Servant? Who walks in darkness and has no light?
Let him trust in the name of the LORD and rely upon
his God.* — Isaiah 50:10

When we arrived back in Hammond, Indiana,
Pastor J and his family graciously opened their
home to us. The plan was that we would stay
there a few days and find a place to rent.

Our purpose for going back to Hammond was to help
with an alternative school that was soon to start up in the
neighborhood high school. I would be the director working
with students who were struggling to continue their
education due to various reasons. Our goal would be to

introduce them to Jesus Who would transform their lives so they could thrive and live happily ever after. It would be funded through a grant that would also give me a decent salary to provide for my family. It was a wonderful plan. However, the Lord had something very different in mind.

A few days passed, and we received word that some of the faculty of the school had adamantly opposed our plans. They had hired an attorney, and in the blink of an eye, an injunction was filed against our plan. It was not going to happen, which meant no grant, no house, and no income for the Anglin family. Tammy and I were dumbfounded, to say the least. We began to intensely pray. We knew the Lord obviously wanted us back in Hammond, but what now?

A precious family heard of our plight and opened a home to us that was in foreclosure. We had hoped to generate enough income to stop that process, but we could not make that happen. For us, during this time, it came down to buying groceries and gas or paying rent. They very kindly allowed us to live there until the bank repossessed the home. Every time there was a knock at the door, we immediately thought, "Will this be a bank representative giving us notice to move out?"

It was hands down the most difficult season that our family had ever walked through. I had not experienced such anguish in all of my Christian walk prior to this. Some nights, I would excuse myself from my family to pray. I would pour out my heart to the Lord and weep until I had no more strength to pray. I felt like I had blown it somewhere, and it seemed there was no answer or recovery from this horrible dark place of sadness. I was so miserable that sometimes it took all the courage I could muster to face another day.

On the morning of April 1st, 2005, my 44th birthday, as I was crawling out of bed, I could see in the very dim light the cold, unfinished block wall in our makeshift bedroom in the basement. A wave of depression nearly bowled me over. I was serving as one of the pastors at the church, and we had early morning prayer every Friday. I had no desire to go that morning. I did not want to be around anyone. Yet, duty was calling. I began to pray and honestly complain to the Lord on my ten-minute drive to the church. I asked the Lord three specific, tearful questions before I arrived at the church. I pulled myself together, as best I could, and entered the building. I found a place in the back of the sanctuary to avoid any pre-prayer conversation.

At the close of the prayer time, we would always gather together and pray. I was hoping that no one would ask about our situation. As we were praying together, Bunny, the lead intercessor of the church, began to speak prophetically to me. I nearly fell over as she addressed all three questions in the same order I had asked the Lord in the car a few minutes before arriving at the church. Never had I received such an affirming and comforting word from the Lord. I deserved a rebuke for my faith breakdown, but I received kind assurance. My faith began to rise again, and the Lord was about to turn the "light" back on in our lives.

I had received an invitation to India from a missionary sometime before that, and I had reapplied for another passport because my previous one had expired. Tammy and Pastor J did not feel good about me taking the trip.

They felt that I was not physically up to it. I took it as a word from the Lord not to go. I remembered a word our dear intercessor friend, Dee Nance, had given me while we were pastoring in Texas. A phrase from the word Dee gave was: "With the passport, comes the favor of the Lord." I found where I had saved it in my computer. Sure enough, that is exactly what Dee had said. That afternoon my passport arrived in the mail.

On a Saturday just prior to the passport arrival, I received three different calls, one from my oldest son, Ryan, another from a concerned brother in the Lord, and a call from our district superintendent of the Indiana Assemblies of God. Amazingly, all three asked me the same question: "Are you willing to pastor again?" When the district superintendent asked me the question, I said, "Well, Pastor, I am now."

The very evening my passport arrived, I received a phone call from Ted. Ted was the pulpit chairman of Faith Assembly of God in Lake Station, Indiana. The church was less than a 15-minute drive from Hammond. When I hung up the phone, I knew in my heart that God was calling us to pastor that church, and later, the unanimous vote of the congregation confirmed it.

In the blink of an eye, God turned our mourning into joyful dancing. The nine months of fiery trial was now finished! We dearly loved the people of the church and our new community. They took better care of us than in anyplace we had ever been before. Our first Christmas there was the most heartwarming that our family has ever experienced together.

REFOCUS

In Hebrews 12:2 it says, "Looking unto Jesus," which can be interpreted as looking away from everything else, and only looking at Jesus. See Him as the One Who will always turn your unbearable trial into ultimate triumph!

REKINDLE

Through that excruciating time of trial and testing, I learned that it is not a time to lie down in anguish and defeat. Rather, it is time to rise in faith and pray with expectation, knowing that God will not allow you to be tempted beyond your ability to stand fast in Him. He will provide you a way of escape that will bring great glory and honor to the Lord Jesus Christ!

REJOICE

The Apostle James started his epistle like this: "My brethren, count it all joy when you fall into various trials." Be very glad. Our great and awesome God will take every single trial and triumph that His children go through and will make it all work for our good. We are His workmanship created in Christ Jesus. He is taking it all and conforming us to the image of His Son! Rejoice with all your heart right now if you trust Him! HALLELUJAH!

REFOCUS

↓

REKINDLE

↓

REJOICE

17

The God Who Never Sleeps

*He will not allow your foot to be moved; He who keeps
you will not slumber. Behold, He who keeps Israel shall
neither slumber nor sleep.*   — Psalm 121:3-4

At our church in Lake Station, Indiana, we invited
Kent Henry, a Christian singer-songwriter, musician, and pastor, to come and speak at a couple of
our services.

After the service the last night he preached, I dropped
him off late at his hotel room. I was very tired when I
came home and was ready to go to sleep. However, as I
laid my head on my pillow, before I could drift off to
sleep, I had an open vision of a horrific car crash.

I saw a vehicle that was so mangled I could not identify
the make of the car. I sat up in my bed and began to pray
intensely in the Spirit. Tammy woke up and asked me

what I was praying about. I told her what I had seen, and assumed the Lord wanted me to pray for the people in the crash, so He would intervene to protect them. I continued to pray for about a half-hour and then the burden lifted.

As soon as I had laid down again to go to sleep, the phone rang. It was my daughter Destiny's best friend, Deborah. There was a tone of nervousness in her voice. She said, "Pastor Tom, everything is okay, but Destiny has been in a car accident. She and the passengers in the other vehicle seem to be fine."

She went on to tell me that the entire right side of the van was damaged, and that it did not look good, but the doors could still open and close. (I made mention of this accident in Chapter 13, "The All-Supplying God.")

Deborah said, "Destiny wanted me to call, because she is busy with the officer filling out the accident report and talking with the other people that were in the accident." I asked her what had happened. She reluctantly said, "Destiny fell asleep at the wheel." I began to thank the Lord for His mercy as I thought of the many accidents that occur frequently on that very busy interstate in Northwest Indiana.

Then it hit me like a ton of bricks! I was shown a terrible accident, burdened to pray, and my youngest daughter was one of the people for whom I was praying. The Lord had shown me what could have happened to her, except, thankfully, He had intervened. How I praised and thanked Him with joy and weeping. Her earthly daddy was about to go to sleep, but her Heavenly Father was wide awake and watchful.

Friends, I could not begin to count the hundreds of

thousands of miles I have logged in my 43-year driving career. Many times I have awakened to find myself in the wrong lane. I have nodded off at the wheel on several solo ministry trips and various other travels. I am not one to believe that God is my co-pilot, but I completely believe He has been, and still is, my pilot. He has kept me and my family safe for many years. I have learned to ask him to do the driving of my entire life. My friends in Romania say it like this: "Duhul Sfânt să facă conducerea," which says, "Let the Holy Spirit do the driving."

There have been many times where His driving has made me nervous, but He knows how to bring us safely home time after time. One glorious day, He will surely transport us to eternal glory, if we trust Him!

REFOCUS

Keep your eyes steadfastly on the One who steadfastly keeps His eyes on you. He never blinks and, much less, never sleeps.

REKINDLE

Ask Him for a greater grace to trust Him with your family and all the other concerns of your life.

REJOICE

Thank Him that He has you and all that pertains to your life in the palm of His hand. Praise Him that He never tires or grows weary of keeping you from all harm. He gives His beloved sleep. Thank Him that you can rest easy because He is going to be up all night watching over you.

REFOCUS

↓

REKINDLE

↓

REJOICE

18

Hidden Treasures

I will go before you and make the crooked places straight;
I will break in pieces the gates of bronze and cut the bars
of iron. I will give you the treasures of darkness and hid-
den riches of secret places, that you may know that I, the
Lord, who call you by your name, am the God of Israel.
— Isaiah 45:2-3

While I was pastoring in Lake Station, Indiana, we invited Pastor Gary Wilkerson, son of the late David Wilkerson, to come minister at our church. As a bonus, he was also bringing his friend, Matthew Ward of the music group, 2nd Chapter of Acts, to minister alongside him. I was so excited. I had met Gary when his dad was starting Times Square Church in New York City in the late 1980s.

On Friday, May 4, 2007, I picked Gary and Matthew

up at the airport. While on the drive back to Lake Station, we talked casually about what was going on in our lives.

In the middle of our conversation, Gary looked at me and said, "Tom, in one year, you are going to know whether you will be here for a long time or a very short time." I said, "That's easy, Gary. I am going to be here for a long time." He just smiled as if to say, "You think so?"

If it had not been Gary Wilkerson who said this to me, I would probably have just blown it off. Instead, I put it on the top shelf of my mind for ready reference. I had absolutely no desire to leave my church or my ministry friends in Lake Station. I was in the middle of a mission field, and there was a life's worth of work before me. Besides, our church took very good care of us. There were so many reasons why I thought I should stay long-term.

Some time later, Tammy and I were at a pastor's retreat with the pastoral team that we were a part of. We were taking some time for individual prayer, and then we were going to meet back in the living room to share and pray together. Carman Garza, wife of my former Teen Challenge associate, Dale Garza, said to me, "Pastor Tom, I have a word for you." I asked her what it was, and she asked me if Isaiah 45:2-3 meant anything to me.

Immediately my spirit leapt inside me. Those two verses had always been my marching orders from the Lord. I knew in my heart the Lord was graciously giving me a heads up that a change was coming, but I was clueless as to what it could be.

After the retreat, I had a real stirring in my heart and began to pray more intensely in the Spirit. One morning, I walked into my office after a lengthy time of prayer, sat down at my desk, and looked at my schedule to see that there were no appointments for the day. I said, "Father, what do you want me to do today?" I heard Him say, "Call Mike McKinney." I said, "I haven't talked to him in a long time. I'll call and see what he is up to."

Mike answered and said, "Tom! I was going to call you today!" I said, "Today? Why today?" He proceeded to tell me that he was praying about resigning his church, which was my home church in North Carolina. My heart sank. Mike was a dear, long-time friend, and Calvary Assembly of God was very dear to my heart. I began my ministry in that church. He began to ask me how to decipher between knowing God was directing you to resign as Pastor, or if it was just your own desire.

Now, I am not the sharpest knife in the drawer, but I began to realize as Mike was talking about resigning, that I was being set up by God. I nervously told him to hang in there, that God would reassure his heart, and he would be happy to continue pastoring within a few days. I tried to quickly get off the phone, but before I could, he asked me if I had an interest in pastoring the church. I struggled with the answer, and I was trying to say "No," but it would not come out of my mouth. I told him that I would be praying for God to direct him and would call him back after he met with his Board.

A few days later, I called him back and asked if he had gotten a word from the Lord regarding his tenure. Mike said immediately, "I sure did!" I said, "So you are staying, right?"

He said confidently, "No, I am going to resign!"

Reluctantly, I said, "Well, you are still the pastor for

now, so if you are so moved, can you mention me to the Board?" Mike said, "I am sure you are familiar with the adage, 'It is easier to ask for forgiveness than permission,' right?" I said, "Brother, what have you done?" He told me that he had already recommended me to the Board and that they wanted to interview me before considering someone else.

The church asked me to come preach so that they could consider me as the next pastor. Tammy and I had a convenient time that we could make the trip, but that timeframe would not work for them. We ended up agreeing to their proposed date, May 4, 2008. That day, the church elected me with a 100 percent vote. I knew then, that I would be at Faith Assembly of God in Lake Station, Indiana, a very short time.

It was exactly one year to the day that Pastor Gary Wilkerson had prophesied to me that I would know in one year whether I would be staying at the church in Lake Station, Indiana, for a long time or a very short time.

Shortly after I had settled in North Carolina, I called Pastor Gary and said, "Brother, please don't prophesy any more surprises for me." We both laughed, and he told me that I was in for another big surprise. Within a few months, our church supernaturally acquired a four-story building with a footprint of over 50,000 square feet!

REFOCUS

Friend, do you feel as though God has a greater mission for you than the one you are in presently? Lift your eyes and see your great big omnipotent Father in Heaven!

REKINDLE

Begin to cry out to God for His absolute will to be done in you. Pray in the Holy Ghost to build your most holy faith. Tell Him, "Here am I, send me!"

REJOICE

God will surely hear you as you earnestly pray. He has a door of ministry for you. Praise Him on your way to that door!

REFOCUS

↓

REKINDLE

↓

REJOICE

19

Faith Fainting Fits

He gives power to the weak, and to those who have no might
He increases strength. — Isaiah 40:29

Several years back, our church was experiencing a tidal wave of incoming expenses. It was wintertime, and the cost of our utilities was through the roof.

Our church property included a four-story building with a footprint of over 50,000 square feet. There were several instances when our electricity was about to be cut off. Needless to say, we were in over our heads. Even the thought of being able to cover all the expenses seemed to be impossible.

I had grown so weary with the weight and burden of trying to pay our bills that I had spent many sleepless nights wrestling with the Lord over our plight, and I was struggling to keep my faith strong. All that pressure had taken a toll on my wife and myself. I remember one morning looking at Tammy and seeing the weariness on her face. A wave of anxiety hit me hard, and I came unglued. I wept until I was in physical pain, and it was difficult to regain my composure. I was angry at myself for leading our church into purchasing this new property. I felt like I had made a decision that was a complete financial failure.

Soon after, I met with our church board to pray for provision for $22,000 to cover expenses, including bills that were past due. We stood in a circle and laid our hands on top of the stack of bills. We began to call on the Lord for miraculous financial help. Betsy, one of our prayer warriors, said, "I just saw Jesus walk up to our prayer circle and lay His hand on top of ours." I said with joy, "He is going to take care of this need!"

And all glory to God, He absolutely did. The very next morning someone sent in a check for $22,000! I would have loved for the trials to have been over after that day, but we were nowhere near that point yet. We continued with impossibility after impossibility. Somehow the Lord always kept us going. Yet, my faith grew more and more fatigued. I was physically and mentally spent.

The next financial burden came when we received a cut-off notice from the power company. We typically did not take up an offering on Wednesday nights, unless there was some type of benevolence need. I purposed in my heart that I would not tell the board that our power would be turned off the next day, and I decided not to ask for a special offering. The power company wanted $6,889 by 2:00 p.m. on Thursday. Otherwise, the power would be turned off.

I thought in my heart, "Well, the power will be terminated tomorrow, and the church will ask me to leave for the mess I've lead them into. That will be the end of it."

I told the church that night that we had a need and to please pray. I further told them that God knew the situation. One of our board members told the treasurer, "I guess there is a monetary need," and left a check for $2,500. The next morning, another member dropped off a check for $2,500. The secretary told me that the church had received $5,000 in total. I told her that was amazing, but we needed another $1,889 to come in before 2:00 p.m. To my amazement, the mailman came by at noon and left a check in the mailbox for $1,900. I made a flying dash to pay the bill before the deadline and returned to the church rejoicing with eleven dollars in my hand!

I could write pages of the many miraculous interventions of the Lord and how He came through right on time. Our most recent miracle regarding our church's financial needs started about six years ago when we were praying about the pressures and financial demands on our church. Ginger Letterman, our lead intercessor, began to prophesy that our church mortgage would be forgiven. We believed the word she spoke, and began to praise the Lord for it in faith. In January of 2018, the mortgage holder forgave the thirty-four remaining years of church mortgage payments. It happened just out of the blue, and we are now debt free by the goodness of God and the kindness and generosity of this benevolent individual.

REFOCUS

Lift your eyes again to the One who holds all things together by the word of His power (see Hebrews 1:3). See the One who specializes in the impossible. Know that when we magnify the greatness of God, He will surely minimize our problems.

REKINDLE

Ask the Lord to give you His fire to fuel your faith. Pray in the Spirit, the unknown tongue. If you are a child of God, you are eligible for the Baptism of the Holy Spirit, which will be evidenced by the gift of an unknown tongue. This is the key to bringing you into the explosive "most holy faith." And remember that we walk by faith and not by sight (2 Corinthians 5:7). With these perilous times that we are living in, we are going to need all the faith that can be generated.

REJOICE

There are endless, mind-boggling miracles to be received for those who believe and receive. The Almighty One, the Creator and Keeper of the universe, is just waiting to give you power in exchange for your weariness. Give Him all the praise and worship that you can pour out on Him. He is so worthy of it all! HALLELUJAH! Can you feel your faith awakened and growing?

20

You Are A Chosen Vessel

You did not choose Me, but I chose you and appointed you that you should go and bear fruit, and that your fruit should remain, that whatever you ask the Father in My name He may give you. — John 15:16

One night many years ago, within the first year of being senior pastor at Burt Assembly of God, I was awakened from sleep, and I heard the Lord say clearly to my heart, "Do also the work of an evangelist."

I thought, "I have recently made the enormous leap from youth pastor to senior pastor, and now You want me to be an evangelist, too?"

After this call, a stirring and a burden for souls began to grip my heart. From that point on, I have been involved in several outreach events throughout the years. The following are a few examples of events where I had the opportunity to share the Gospel. I pray they will encourage you to step out in your faith and share the Good News with others.

On my second trip to Romania, we went to a village outside the town where the church was located in which we were ministering. There was no true Gospel being preached there, but over 175 people gathered for the open-air event we held. I preached and gave the invitation for salvation, but no one moved. I told the interpreter to invite them again to come forward and surrender to Jesus as Savior and Lord. Still, to my astonishment, no one came. I urged the interpreter to tell them one more time.

When Cristina, the interpreter, spoke to the crowd again, an old man walking with a cane began to come forward. When the old man got about halfway to the front, he was nearly stampeded by the rest of the people coming forward to repent and believe the Gospel. I found out later that it was almost the entire population of that little village who came to Christ that day.

In Hammond, Indiana, we launched a crisis intervention office for Teen Challenge, where I began to see numerous souls come to Christ. Tammy and I also led the Caring Hands ministry there at Hammond First Assembly of God. Caring Hands had been established in the church for quite some time. Every Saturday, we fed and gave groceries to the homeless and local families in need. I would always share a brief Gospel message with them, and in the two years we ran it, I prayed with well over 200 individuals to come to Jesus.

During this time, we were invited to be the evangelists for an event called "Compassion 2001." It was hosted by the Hammond church. I was asked to speak because of my role as Executive Director of InnerMission Teen Challenge. This was important because we were working with other churches to come together to reach out to our very impoverished community.

Over 2,500 people came that day to the event, due in part to the free medical and dental services being provided. Those who came also received free food, clothing, marital and family counseling, along with other free services.

The entryway to have access to the event to obtain the needed services was to first come through an open-sided tent. The tent seated 147 people total. I preached a total of seventeen ten-minute messages as each group came in, one group at a time. Over 1,000 people, many of them of gang affiliation, signed cards that they had surrendered to Jesus Christ as Lord and Savior that day.

We also did an outreach in Gary, Indiana, the city next door to Hammond. We gave the invitation to surrender to Jesus as Lord and Savior. We told only the people who had come to Christ for the first time that they could have a Bible. We had 350 Bibles total. We gave them all away, and many people still came in asking for Bibles.

And, lastly, since our move back home to Western North Carolina in 2008, I have had the glorious privilege of praying with over 250 inmates to come to Christ as Lord and Savior in the prison where I have been ministering over the last nine years. With just event-based evangelism, there have been over 2,000 souls won to Christ, as well as many one-on-one salvations through the years.

In Christ alone, I will boast. I am just a vessel that He has chosen, just a brand snatched from the flames of Hell where I was headed. Friend, in Christ, you too are a chosen vessel of the most-high God. How awesome are the things He has prepared for those that will dare to yield entirely to His Great Holy Spirit.

REFOCUS

Lift your eyes again to Jesus, the Author and Finisher of your faith. See Him as the One with a blueprint for your life spread out on His strategy table. You are personally invited by the all-wise God to play a major role in His end time, Kingdom plan! Keep your eyes fixed on Him until it becomes a crystal-clear vision before your eyes.

REKINDLE

Begin to pray as if everything God has in store for you is depending on your passionate praying. Someone wise once said, "A funny thing happens when we don't pray ... NOTHING!" Ask the Lord to light a fire of praying in the Spirit inside your heart! And P.U.S.H. – Pray Until Something Happens.

REJOICE

For those of you in Jesus Christ, let your praise and worship gush from your heart and through your lips to Him Who is altogether lovely, altogether worthy, and has your life's plan altogether. Praise Him Who is altogether able to do exceedingly, abundantly above all you can even ask or imagine! Thank Him for calling and choosing you to show forth the praises of Him who has called you out of darkness into His marvelous light! HALLELUJAH!

21

The Power Of Letting Go

And when Jesus had cried out with a loud voice, He said, "Father, into Your hands I commit My spirit." Having said this, He breathed His last. — Luke 23:46

A very tiring and scorching July day in 1999 was coming to an end. I had just finished unloading a large U-Haul truck with the help of some new friends in Hammond, Indiana. I was driving back across town to my temporary dwelling place with my wife, Tammy, and our four children.

With a thirteen-hour drive in front on me, I was thinking, "Lord, I believe I have done the right thing in coming here, but there sure are a great deal of unknowns in this new land. I know that you can work all the details out, Lord, and You will have to because it's over my head now."

A song playing faintly on the radio caught my ear:

"You've got to let go and let God be God." The words rang like a bell in my soul. It was as though the Holy Spirit was giving me the key to success in this new assignment by way of a song that I had never heard before.

Through my walk with the Lord, I have found so much joy and peace by simply letting go and letting God be God. When we let go of our plans, our purposes, and our agendas, God begins to establish His plan, purpose, and agenda in our lives. I believe this is what every true child of God really wants, which is to let go.

However, the choice to let go may be a little easier said than done at times. But when God is in it, it is always visited with POWER. As a family, we have walked through some great difficulties, but we committed our way to Jesus, and He has never once failed us to this very day.

Allow me to share something with you that the wonderful people of The Bridge Church of Western North Carolina (WNC) are very accustomed to—my usage of acrostics. I will be using the acrostic for the phrase "LET GO" to conclude this book.

L - *LOOSE*
E - *ENTRUST*
T - *THANKSGIVING*
G - *GAMBLE*
O - *ONWARD*

LOOSE

Acts 27:39-40 says, "When it was day, they did not recognize the land; but they observed a bay with a beach, onto which they planned to run the ship if possible. And they let go the anchors and left them in the sea, meanwhile loosing the rudder ropes; and they hoisted the mainsail to the wind and made for shore."

Perhaps you are familiar with the account of the prison ship voyage of the Apostle Paul. He tried to talk the captain out of the voyage because he knew it would be no pleasure cruise. Hurricane Euroclydon nearly took the ship down into the depths of the sea. Long story short, Paul got hold of God, the ship was absolutely destroyed, yet all the lives were mercifully spared. They turned the control over to the sea and ultimately to the Lord. Do you see it? They let go and "loosed" their control.

Psalm 77:19 says, "Your way was in the sea, Your path in the great waters, and Your footsteps were not known." They found the way of God in the storm, and so will you, when you make your desperate cry to Him and put all your trust in your Heavenly Captain.

ENTRUST

Matthew 27:50-53 says, "And Jesus cried out again with a loud voice, and yielded up His spirit. (Luke 23:46: "… Father, 'into Your hands I commit My spirit.'") Then, behold, the veil of the temple was torn in two from top to the bottom; and the earth quaked, and the rocks were split, and the graves were opened; and many bodies of the saints who had fallen asleep were raised; and coming out of the graves after His resurrection, they went into the holy city, and appeared to many."

Jesus, in His last seconds of life, entrusted His spirit to His Father. He yielded and let go of His life, and His action invoked the mighty power of God. The earth quaked, and out of Jesus' death, life filled the departed saints. His action has brought abundant, eternal life to untold millions. There are faith actions that you and I can take that will stir the heart of our Father and cause His mighty presence to manifest! Psalm 68:8 states: "The earth shook; the heavens also dropped rain at the presence of God; Sinai itself was moved at the presence of God, the God of Israel."

THANKSGIVING

Acts 16:25-26 says, "But at midnight Paul and Silas were praying and singing hymns to God, and the prisoners were listening to them. Suddenly there was a great earthquake, so that the foundations of the prison were shaken; and immediately all the doors were opened and everyone's chains were loosed."

Perhaps one of the greatest indicators that we have truly "let go" is when we can praise and worship our God in the darkest hour of trial and persecution. Paul and Silas were way too deeply in love with the Lord to let a little beating, shackles, and imprisonment dampen their love for Jesus, even if they were on death row. God always has and always will show up when praise and worship go up.

GAMBLE

1 Samuel 14:6, 12-15 says, "Then Jonathan said to the young man who bore his armor, 'Come, let us go over to the garrison of these uncircumcised; it may be that the Lord will work for us. For nothing restrains the Lord from saving by many or by few.' ... Then the men of the garrison called to Jonathan and his armorbearer, and said, 'Come

up to us, and we will show you something.' Jonathan said to his armorbearer, 'Come up after me, for the Lord has delivered them into the hand of Israel.' And Jonathan climbed up on his hands and knees with his armorbearer after him; and they fell before Jonathan. And as he came after him, his armorbearer killed them. That first slaughter which Jonathan and his armorbearer made was about twenty men within about half an acre of land. And there was trembling in the camp, in the field, and among all the people. The garrison and the raiders also trembled; and the earth quaked, so that it was a very great trembling."

Child of God, faith will always involve risk. Faith is indeed a gamble, but true faith will always stack the deck in our favor. When we stick our neck out for the honor and glory of our great God, the greatness of God manifests in Almighty power. His Presence will always cause a quaking in the enemy's camp. God will absolutely not sit still on His throne when His beloved children charge the enemy. He will bring about a mighty victory. As we lay down our lives for the same cause for which Jesus laid down His life, the salvation of souls, His Presence comes to assure the victory!

ONWARD

Acts 4:29-31 says, "'Now, Lord, look on their threats, and grant to Your servants that with all boldness they may speak Your word, by stretching out Your hand to heal, and that signs and wonders may be done through the name of Your holy Servant Jesus.'

"And when they had prayed, the place where they were assembled together was shaken; and they were all filled with the Holy Spirit, and they spoke the word of God with boldness."

When the notable miracle shook all those that knew the lame beggar at the Beautiful gate that day, it really shook things up. The blind Pharisees were outraged.

They worked so hard to rid the people of Israel of this "impostor" Jesus Christ. This miracle of healing had taken place by way of the name of Jesus, and because of this, the disciples were charged by the high priest, the rulers, and the elders of Israel not to speak anymore in His name. Jesus' followers determined to keep following Him, so they called a prayer meeting and cried out to the Lord for strength to press on. Hallelujah, their petitions were granted, and the presence of God shook the building to let them know, "Onward, Christian Soldiers, for I Am with you always!"

REFOCUS

My friend, lift your eyes once more and see Him who knows no retreat or defeat. As you have purposed to go on with Him, He has purposed to lead you into greater and greater triumphs through and for His Son. Look unto Him and be radiant, for you will never be put to shame (See Psalm 34:5).

REKINDLE

Fall on your knees and cry out to the Lord like Elijah did on that very historical day on Mount Carmel. Ask Him to let His fire fall on you and burn away all that is not of Him. Ask Him to set on fire your faith in Him and

love for Him. Ask Him for a mighty fire upon your life—
fire to light up the cold, dark world around you.

REJOICE

Child of God, I am so excited for you! If you are
following hard and going hard after the Lord, an unprece-
dented transformation is coming upon you. Praise Him,
thank Him, and worship Him like you believe it. Hallelujah,
in believing it, you shall surely receive it!

REFOCUS

↓

REKINDLE

↓

REJOICE

FINALE

Dear Reader,

I am greatly humbled that you have read to this point. Thank you! My simple prayer is that these true testimonies have somehow awakened the measure of faith God has given you. I pray that you will allow the Holy Spirit to lead you into a giant faith that will bring much joy to the Father's heart. I pray your heart is stirred to love the Lord even more than ever! JESUS IS EVERYTHING, AND HE IS KING! TO HIM BE ALL THE HONOR, GLORY, AND POWER FOREVER AND EVER!

I am joyfully His and yours! Every blessing to you in our Lord Jesus Christ! Amen!

— Tom Anglin, Lead Pastor
The Bridge Church of WNC
Spruce Pine, NC

ABOUT THE AUTHOR

PASTORS TOM AND TAMMY ANGLIN

TOM ANGLIN began preaching in 1982 and pastoring in 1986. He has an extensive history in ministry that includes pastoring seven churches and founding a Teen Challenge Center for Boys. He has ministered in Romania and Uganda. He is a prison evangelist, a law enforcement chaplain, and is a "Prison Volunteer of the Year" recipient.

Pastor Anglin's passion is winning and discipling souls, exhorting God's people, and calling the body of Christ to come together. He has preached open air to 2,500 in Hammond, Indiana, one day, where one thousand souls came to Christ. He preached open air in Romania, where nearly the entire village came to Christ and a church was planted. He preached open air in Gary, Indiana, one day, and over 350 came to faith in Christ. In the last ten years of preaching in a local prison, over 250 have come to Christ.

Pastor Tom has been married to Tammy King Anglin for over 38 years. They have four children—Ryan, Sarah, Destiny, and Tyler; six grandchildren, with two more on the way. They reside in Western North Carolina. Learn more at his website: www.TomAnglin.com

www.ingramcontent.com/pod-product-compliance
Lightning Source LLC
Chambersburg PA
CBHW051429090426
42737CB00014B/2890